Building Polyfills
Web Platform APIs for the Present and Future

Brandon Satrom

Beijing · Cambridge · Farnham · Köln · Sebastopol · Tokyo

Building Polyfills

by Brandon Satrom

Printed in the United States of America.

Published by O'Reilly Media, Inc., 1005 Gravenstein Highway North, Sebastopol, CA 95472.

O'Reilly books may be purchased for educational, business, or sales promotional use. Online editions are also available for most titles (*http://my.safaribooksonline.com*). For more information, contact our corporate/institutional sales department: 800-998-9938 or *corporate@oreilly.com*.

Editors: Simon St. Laurent and Brian Anderson	**Cover Designer:** Randy Comer
Production Editor: Nicole Shelby	**Interior Designer:** David Futato
Proofreader: Sharon Wilkey	**Illustrator:** Rebecca Demarest

February 2014:   First Edition

Revision History for the First Edition:

2014-02-14:   First release

See *http://oreilly.com/catalog/errata.csp?isbn=9781449370732* for release details.

ISBN: 978-1-449-37073-2

[LSI]

Table of Contents

Preface

If you play a game of word association with a room full of frontend developers, *polyfill* will no doubt receive mention from more than a few participants. This word—traditionally a synonym for *fallback, spackle,* or *patch*—was unfamiliar to many developers until just a few years ago, but has become a staple of conversations about modern and open web technologies. And while polyfilling has traditionally operated as a practice for delivering modern features to nonmodern browsers (*oldIE*, meaning IE6–8, is increasingly a synonym for older browsers), the concept has expanded over the last few years to include the addition of new and experimental platform features to all browsers, including the newest and most cutting-edge.

Before our eyes, the practice of polyfilling is evolving from an adoption technique to a full-blown design pattern that allows developers to "spackle" their browsers with whatever semantics they wish. AngularJS, a very popular and fast-growing app framework, encourages this practice by enabling developers to use directives to add custom HTML tags and components to their applications.

Design by polyfill extends beyond frameworks as well. One such example is the Web Components effort, a set of specifications in the W3C designed to make the creation of custom semantics and encapsulated components a feature in the browser itself. With Web Components, if you want a `<calendar>` component, you need only create one yourself, or grab one from a third party. It's a powerful idea, and if the concept takes off, it will unlock a new set of capabilities for web developers while adding new depth and richness to the applications we create.

Who This Book Is For

When it comes to the art of patching browser capabilities via polyfills, developers fall into two camps: those *using* polyfills to provide modern web platform capabilities in their sites, and those *building* polyfills for the broader web community. The book is primarily focused on the latter camp, and is intended to serve as an introduction to polyfilling, to provide a set of principles and practical guidelines for building *reliable polyfills*, and finally, to provide a road map for the future of polyfilling itself. However, even if you're a JavaScript developer not especially interested in building polyfills, there's a lot of useful content in this book in the realm of test-driven development (TDD), JavaScript build workflows, and performance optimizations.

At present, countless articles and book chapters exist that cover the subject of polyfilling. However, in nearly every case, these articles are targeted at polyfill consumers, not the intrepid developers who build these libraries. One notable exception is Addy Osmani's guide for polyfill developers (*http://bit.ly/osmani-guide*), an introductory read that I highly recommend. Beyond Addy's article, there are few resources, online or in print, that cover the topic of polyfills from the viewpoint of the developer. A lack of definitive resources for building these libraries means that we must strike out on our own, or slowly dig through other libraries for patterns and ideas.

My sincere hope is that this book will close the gap by serving as a field guide for polyfill developers. We'll start with a cursory introduction to polyfilling on the web platform, and I'll share some principles and guidelines for building polyfills that developers can rely on. Once the guidelines have been established, we'll shift the discussion to an in-depth walk-through of building a real-life, reasonably complex polyfills.

Once I've covered the ins and outs of building polyfills, the last two chapters will shift to focus on that emerging trend on the web platform: the *forward polyfill*, or *prollyfill*. This pattern, as I've mentioned already, enables developers to test and work with emerging concepts, sometimes ahead of the browser vendors themselves. By the time we're done, you'll have all the tools you need to build reliable polyfills for the present, and the future, of the Web.

How This Book Is Organized

This book is organized into two parts. In the first part, we discuss the ins and outs of polyfill development, starting with the current landscape of polyfilling in Chapter 1. In Chapter 2, I'll introduce some principles and practices for the polyfill developer, guidance that I hope you'll find useful regardless of the type of polyfill you plan to build. Then, in Chapters 3 through 5, we'll dig deep into polyfill development with a real-life library. In Chapter 3, I'll introduce our sample project, an HTML5 Forms polyfill, and we'll build out several features for this library. In Chapter 4, we'll talk about testing and build workflows, and I'll introduce you to some tools that can make your life easier as a polyfill developer. Finally, we'll wrap up Part I with a discussion on polyfill performance in Chapter 5, where I'll walk through a couple of cases in which we can improve the speed of our polyfill.

In Part II of this book, we'll turn our focus to the future of polyfilling, the *prollyfill*. In Chapter 6, I'll introduce the concept of prollyfilling and walk through examples of this important variation on the polyfill. Finally, in Chapter 7, we'll close out the book with another walk-through and build a prollyfill for a cutting-edge web platform specification. Once we're done, you should be well equipped to jump into the present, and future, of polyfilling.

Conventions Used in This Book

The following typographical conventions are used in this book:

Italic
> Indicates new terms, URLs, email addresses, filenames, and file extensions.

`Constant width`
> Used for program listings, as well as within paragraphs to refer to program elements such as variable or function names, databases, data types, environment variables, statements, and keywords.

`Constant width bold`
> Shows commands or other text that should be typed literally by the user.

`Constant width italic`
> Shows text that should be replaced with user-supplied values or by values determined by context.

This element signifies a tip or suggestion.

This element signifies a general note.

This element indicates a warning or caution.

Using Code Examples

Supplemental material (code examples, exercises, etc.) is available for download at *http://bit.ly/kendo-ui* and *http://bit.ly/slacker-js*.

This book is here to help you get your job done. In general, if example code is offered with this book, you may use it in your programs and documentation. You do not need to contact us for permission unless you're reproducing a significant portion of the code. For example, writing a program that uses several chunks of code from this book does not require permission. Selling or distributing a CD-ROM of examples from O'Reilly books does require permission. Answering a question by citing this book and quoting example code does not require permission. Incorporating a significant amount of example code from this book into your product's documentation does require permission.

We appreciate, but do not require, attribution. An attribution usually includes the title, author, publisher, and ISBN. For example: "*Building Polyfills* by Brandon Satrom (O'Reilly). Copyright 2014 Brandon Satrom, 978-1-449-37073-2."

If you feel your use of code examples falls outside fair use or the permission given above, feel free to contact us at *permissions@oreilly.com*.

Safari® Books Online

 *Safari Books Online* is an on-demand digital library that delivers expert content in both book and video form from the world's leading authors in technology and business.

Technology professionals, software developers, web designers, and business and creative professionals use Safari Books Online as their primary resource for research, problem solving, learning, and certification training.

Safari Books Online offers a range of product mixes and pricing programs for organizations, government agencies, and individuals. Subscribers have access to thousands of books, training videos, and prepublication manuscripts in one fully searchable database from publishers like O'Reilly Media, Prentice Hall Professional, Addison-Wesley Professional, Microsoft Press, Sams, Que, Peachpit Press, Focal Press, Cisco Press, John Wiley & Sons, Syngress, Morgan Kaufmann, IBM Redbooks, Packt, Adobe Press, FT Press, Apress, Manning, New Riders, McGraw-Hill, Jones & Bartlett, Course Technology, and dozens more. For more information about Safari Books Online, please visit us online.

How to Contact Us

Please address comments and questions concerning this book to the publisher:

O'Reilly Media, Inc.
1005 Gravenstein Highway North
Sebastopol, CA 95472
800-998-9938 (in the United States or Canada)
707-829-0515 (international or local)
707-829-0104 (fax)

We have a web page for this book, where we list errata, examples, and any additional information. You can access this page at *http://bit.ly/building-polyfills*.

To comment or ask technical questions about this book, send email to *bookques tions@oreilly.com*.

For more information about our books, courses, conferences, and news, see our website at *http://www.oreilly.com*.

Find us on Facebook: *http://facebook.com/oreilly*

Follow us on Twitter: *http://twitter.com/oreillymedia*

Watch us on YouTube: *http://www.youtube.com/oreillymedia*

Acknowledgments

First and foremost, thanks go to my wife Sarah, whose faith in me is equal parts unflagging and humbling. I am ever grateful for her encouragement to take on these kinds of projects, while also keeping me honest and engaged with my family. It is because of her that I don't have to apologize for countless nights of missed dinners and time lost with our family, because no such sacrifice was required. I hope you'll agree that the quality of this work did not suffer, as a result.

I'm also grateful to my boys, Benjamin and Jack, whose smiles and playful spirits remind me of what really matters each and every day. Thanks for all of the writing interruptions for hugs and kisses, boys! Also, to Matthew Satrom. Though this book was completed before you were born, you were constantly in my thoughts. I can't wait to meet you in early 2014!

Thanks also to my fantastic colleagues at Telerik, especially Burke Holland, who reviewed every single line of this book, ran and critiqued all of the code samples, and provided immensely helpful feedback when I was deep in the weeds of polyfilling. Thanks also to Addy Osmani who, in addition to writing the foreword, provided early input on the proposal and table of contents for this book. Any "aha!" moments you have while reading this book are due to the insight of these two gentlemen, while any exclamations to the opposite effect are solely the fault of its author.

I also want to thank Brian Kardell for his helpful insights about the origin of the term "prollyfill" and his work on both HitchJS and as chair of the Extensible Web W3C Community Group. Thanks for all of your hard work extending the Web forward, Brian.

Finally, I want to thank my editors, Simon St. Laurent and Brian Anderson. This project started as a vision in Simon's head, and I'm grateful to have been given the opportunity to turn that vision into reality. I am grateful to have had Simon's keen insight, experience, and guidance early on in this project. Brian helped shepherd this project from its very raw stages all the way through to the end, and I am in his debt for keeping things on track, helping me manage my deadlines, and driving this book to completion. Thank you both.

Foreword

Polyfill, a word synonymous with fallback, is a term which has become all too familiar with developers building modern web apps targeting nonmodern browsers. In the past, however, much of the guidance around authoring them was limited to out of date resources, often leaving developers to fend for their own.

I'm happy to say that the lack of a definitive resource for learning how to build robust polyfills is filled by this excellent book, allowing you to spend less time striking out on your own and more time building a reliable solution that won't let you down.

In this practical guide, you will be shown through the fundamental principles and guidelines for building polyfills that users can rely on. Learn how to responsibly match the APIs specified by the web platform features you're targeting and deliver a solution which is focused and does one thing well. It can be a challenge to understand the ins and outs of platform features, but this guide cuts through the nonsense, helping you understand web platform features so that you can deliver complete polyfills which won't frustrate developers.

In the fast-paced world of frontend development, polyfills are no longer strictly used for delivering modern features to older browsers, but also to enable developers to use experimental platform features. This hints at the potential for polyfills to be around far longer than when all browsers become evergreen (or auto-updating).

Walk through an introduction to polyfilling, discover the core principles for building reliable polyfills, and then move on to an in-depth explanation of developing a real-world, nontrivial polyfill—the HTML5 Forms polyfill. Brandon talks about emerging trends such as the "experimental feature" polyfill and how this has been a successful pattern for W3C specifications like Web Components, encompassing Custom Elements, HTML Imports, and other technologies.

Building Polyfills is an invaluable resource which will teach you lessons that can be easily reused to write reliable polyfills today and in the future. I found it filled with useful best practices, original thinking, and pro-tips that make it an important reference book for anyone serious about writing cross-browser polyfills.

— Addy Osmani, Chrome Developer Relations

PART I

Building Polyfills

In this first part, we'll explore the world of polyfills as they exist today. In Chapter 1, we'll discuss the origin of polyfilling, and in Chapter 2 I'll share some principles and practices for the polyfill developer to consider when building libraries for cross-browser compatability. In Chapters 3 through 5, we'll get our hands dirty and walk through building a polyfill for the HTML5 Forms specification. We'll also cover testing and build workflows and the all-important subject of polyfill performance.

CHAPTER 1

The Current State of Web Polyfills

Like many things in the world of technology, the practice of *polyfilling* is far older than its name. And even though the term itself is a recent addition to the web platform canon, as long as we've had multiple browsers with varying and inconsistent implementations of web platform features—which is to say, always—we've had the practice of polyfilling in one form or another. Every developer who mucks with the string prototype to add a `trim()` function for oldIE is creating a polyfill, as is the developer who lovingly adds a homegrown `window.addEventListner()` function to IE8 in the hopes of simplifying her event management code. As a practice, polyfilling has been around for a while, but its naming coincides with a time in which its use on the Web exploded: the advent of HTML5.

Polyfilling: Past, Present, and Future

Much as the term *Ajax* was minted at a time when JavaScript and XHR apps were a daily occurrence, the practice of polyfilling was given a name at a time when developers were increasingly looking at HTML5 and thinking, "How can I get some of that in my site?" Part of the answer at the time was polyfilling and, in many ways, it's been an adequate answer. For the last several years, polyfilling has allowed developers to target multiple browsers with new technologies, while not leaving those oldIE users behind. This is polyfilling's past, and also its present. We still live in a world where the predominant use case for a polyfill is "filling the gaps" in a browser that doesn't yet natively provide a feature or features that we need.

But were that the end of the story, I don't think an entire book on polyfills would be very interesting. Thankfully, the story continues, and a subtle shift in how we look at polyfilling is taking place in the web community. Rather than simply building polyfills to modernize older browsers, a new class of library is starting to emerge. These libraries, sometimes called *forward polyfills*, or *prollyfills*, are created with the goal of trying out new ideas and unproven specifications on the Web. This can be something as simple as a library that adds classes to JavaScript in accordance with the ECMAScript 6 specification, or as complex as a full suite of libraries that provide advance support for Web Components, as is the case with the Polymer project (*http://polymer-project.org*).

It's a powerful pattern, and this new class of polyfill is shifting the balance of power on the Web. Increasingly, these libraries are allowing us lowly web developers to emerge as not just authors of websites and applications, but also as architects of the web platform itself. It's an exciting time to be a polyfiller.

What Is a Polyfill (and What Is It Not)?

In 2009, as he was working on the popular book *Introducing HTML5*, Remy Sharp conceived and coined the term *polyfill* to describe a practice that he'd seen increasingly applied by developers adopting HTML5 and CSS3 in their applications. In a post on his blog (*http://bit.ly/remysharp*) from 2010, Sharp defines the term as follows:

> A polyfill, or polyfiller, is a piece of code (or plug-in) that provides the technology that you, the developer, expect the browser to provide natively. Flattening the API landscape if you will.

For those of you in the United Kingdom, the term *polyfill* might evoke images of Polyfilla, a paste that Britons use to cover cracks and holes in wall (we call this *spackling* in the United States). It's a convenient image that happens to describe exactly what good polyfills strive to do: fill in the gaps and holes of browsers so that a developer can go to work on a smooth, consistent surface.

The term also has a more direct, deeper meaning if analyzed in parts, *poly* and *fill*. *Fill* denotes the hole in the browser that the library exists to address, and *poly* means that the problem can be solved by using any number of techniques. JavaScript might be the predominant polyfilling approach, but there are several examples of polyfills that fall back to plug-ins like Silverlight or Flash to provide functionality to the browser. Notable examples of these are the excanvas plug-in (*http://bit.ly/xcanvas*), which falls back to Silverlight to provide Canvas support in IE6–8 and mediaelement.js (*http://mediaele mentjs.com/*), which provides consistent HTML5 media support across browsers with Flash.

According to Sharp, the practice that we now refer to as polyfilling needed a new term because existing terms didn't convey the key idea of replicating the API of native browser features by using JavaScript. Polyfills are distinct from both *shimming* and *progressive enhancement* in that regard. The term *shim* does describe a library or bit of code that adds features or functionality to the browser, and may even provide an abstraction that spans cross-browser inconsistencies, but these libraries often introduce their own, specialized APIs. jQuery, which was first introduced as a way to normalize Document Object Model (DOM) interactions across browsers, is a popular example of a shim.

Progressive enhancement and its cousin graceful degradation are also inadequate for this idea, as these terms imply building sites that either gain functionality with JavaScript, or that remain functional in the absence of JavaScript, respectively. Polyfills often depend on JavaScript in the absence of native browser functionality and, as such, neither of these terms seem appropriate.

When Remy Sharp conceived of the term *polyfill*, he wasn't attempting to coin a new phrase for posterity. Instead, he was hoping to describe an increasingly relevant practice that would undoubtedly become even more important as HTML5 and the open Web continued to proliferate throughout the development world. The web development community needed a term to describe this burgeoning practice, and Sharp had one to offer. In spite of periodic assertions from corners of the community that the word should be changed, "polyfilling" has caught on. I don't expect that it, or the practice that it represents, will go anywhere any time soon. Quite the opposite, in fact, which is why you hold this book in your hands.

Types of Polyfills

With a proper explanation of polyfills out of the way, let's spend a few moments talking about types of polyfills. While the formal definition does have a pure, simple interpretation, polyfills, in reality, don't always respect this definition to a T. In this section, we'll look at some common "classes" of polyfills, as well as the pros and cons of choosing each approach when building polyfills of your own.

The Shim

A *shim* is not a polyfill, at least by definition, but is often considered a worthy member of the polyfilling conversation nonetheless. This is for two reasons:

1. People often use the two terms interchangeably.
2. Shims and polyfills share similar goals, in spite of their differing approaches.

A shim is a piece of code, typically JavaScript, that's designed to add functionality into the browser that is not already present, or to bring a level of consistency to various browser implementations. Unlike the various polyfill types, shims do not map their functionality to a built-in or specified browser API, instead choosing to implement their own API that developers must learn and adopt in order to leverage provided functionality.

As stated previously, jQuery—specifically the library's sizzle selector engine and event management functionality—is a classic example of a shim. Selecting an element from the DOM with jQuery requires a specific action on the part of the developer. For instance, consider the simple selector in Example 1-1.

Example 1-1. Using jQuery to interact with the DOM

```
$('#myTodoList').find('li.dueToday')
  .css('background-color','yellow')
  .end()
  .find('li.overdue')
  .css('background-color', 'red');
```

The preceding sample is doing a number of things, not the least of which is performing three separate element selections from the DOM. This code is guaranteed to work consistently across all browsers, from IE6 on up, and there's nothing special I need to do to manage how jQuery performs this selection from one browser to the next. Internally, jQuery does manage a complex algorithm for DOM selection based on the browser, using HTML5's querySelector/querySelectorAll syntax, if supported, or the classic document.GetElementById/document.GetElementsByClassName approach, if not. However, because all of this functionality is abstracted into a separate API from that specified by the W3C—as opposed to adding its functionality to the document object prototype—it fits more into the definition of a shim than that of a polyfill.

In spite of the fact that shims are not polyfills, they do still offer some advantages to developers. For starters, their opt-in nature means that developers leveraging their functionality aren't doing so by accident. Instead they are choosing to learn a new API because the library provides needed functionality. Because a library-specific API is being used, developers are guaranteed not to override built-in browser functionality in an unexpected way, which can happen with pure polyfills. A developer adopting a shim (hopefully) knows what he's getting himself into and has chosen that shim for a reason.

Another advantage to shims is that the library developer isn't constrained by the specified API of built-in functionality. If the developer wishes to diverge from the API to improve the library's interface for developers—for instance, the chainability of jQuery selectors and methods—she is free to do so without worrying about affecting or breaking a standardized API. With pure polyfills, respecting the API is vital, as we'll discuss in Chapter 2.

While some see the opt-in nature of shims as an advantage, others disagree. To these developers, adopting a shim is akin to taking on technical debt that requires rework to remove. Imagine a developer who adopts a shim with the goal of gaining some as-yet unimplemented functionality in the browser. If, in the future, the browsers add this native functionality, the developer must remove or update the shim to offer the native experience—and concomitant performance gains—to the end user. As long as the shim remains in place, the end user will receive a less than ideal experience in their perfectly capable browser. Polyfills, on the other hand, tend to have a built-in answer to this problem.

The Opt-In Polyfill

The next polyfill type on our list is the *opt-in polyfill*. These libraries qualify as polyfills in the sense that they operate on standard APIs. However, they are *opt-in* because the developer must take action in order to leverage them in their apps.

As an example, consider PIE (*http://bit.ly/pie-poly*), a popular CSS3 polyfill. PIE, aka *Progressive Internet Explorer*, exists to provide CSS3 features like border-radius, box-shadow, and border-image to, you guessed it, IE6, 7, and 8. The library works in one of two ways. Developers can use the relevant CSS properties, as normal, and then opt into PIE by including a behavior property at the end of the CSS rule, as shown in Example 1-2.

Example 1-2. Activate PIE using CSS

```
#myElement {
  background: #DDD;
  padding: 2em;
  -o-border-radius: 1em;
  -moz-border-radius: 1em;
  -webkit-border-radius: 1em;
  border-radius: 1em;
  **`behavior: url(PIE.htc);`** ❶
}
```

❶   This IE-specific line of CSS activates the PIE polyfill.

In this example, the opt-in happens when the browser's parser encounters the behavior property. If the behavior property looks foreign to you, you're not alone. This property, which is supported only in Internet Explorer 5.5 through 9, allows you to use CSS to add a script to a selector, with the purpose of implementing something Microsoft calls HTML components (*http://bit.ly/html-dhtml*). The .htc extension on our PIE file is an HTML component-specific format that's essentially markup and JavaScript, plus some additional vendor-specific elements that define the components themselves.

When loaded, *PIE.htc* uses the CSS properties defined in its loading selector—border-radius in this case—to fake those features using the HTC component. So, PIE is using a decade-old IE-specific hack in order to add support for CSS3 to IE6–8. That's pretty clever! Not only that; it's also efficient. Since other browsers don't support the behavior property, its existence will be overlooked, and the HTC file will be neither loaded nor parsed by browsers that already support CSS3 properties.

If the thought of using DHTML to fake CSS3 support in IE isn't your cup o' tea, you can also use JavaScript to add PIE to your apps, as illustrated in Example 1-3. Of course, you'll still need to define the CSS for border-radius, as well as include any of PIE's dependencies, like jQuery.

Example 1-3. Activate PIE using JavaScript

```
Modernizr.load({
  test: Modernizr.borderradius,
  nope: 'PIE.js',
  complete: function() {
    if (window.PIE) {
      // Select all elements with class 'rounded'
      $('.rounded').each(function() {
        PIE.attach(this);
      });
    }
  }
});
```

In this example, we start by leveraging Modernizr's built-in `Modernizr.load` capabilities to determine if the CSS3 `border-radius` property is supported. A key feature of `Modernizr.load` is the ability to conditionally load a script file based on the truthiness or falsiness of a test. When using polyfills, it's important to consider the users who don't need a polyfill just as much as those who do. Ideally, you never want to load a library that a user doesn't need, and polyfills are no exception. With `Modernizr.load`, you can load libraries only when the browser requires them.

 Hopefully, you're familiar with Modernizr (*http://modernizr.com*) as a polyfill consumer. If not, I highly recommend learning the library since, as a polyfill author, you'll need to be intimately familiar with the various ways developers perform feature detection before loading your library. That is, unless you do the feature detection for them, which we'll discuss shortly.

Once *PIE.js* is loaded, the `complete` function is called. At this point, I opt in to PIE by selecting elements from the DOM via jQuery and passing each element into the `PIE.attach` function, which does the fancy corner-rounding for me. It's a bit more code than the HTML Components approach, but still simple enough to implement.

Opt-in polyfills have a couple of advantages over shims. For starters, these libraries work against standard APIs, meaning that developers don't have to learn a new API or write a bunch of needless boilerplate in order to use them. What's more, the footprint of these libraries is relatively small and self-contained. When the developer no longer needs to support an opt-in polyfill, the offending code is easy to track down and remove.

On the other hand, opt-in polyfills do still introduce technical debt in the form of extra code, even if that code is often just a few lines. A line or two of extra code is all fine and good with example code, but imagine having to add opt-in support for a few hundred selectors across a large site. Now, imagine what it would be like to remove all of that opt-in code a few years down the road, and deal with the regression that would undoubtedly pop up. Doesn't sound like much fun, does it? Thankfully, there are other approaches that are designed to be a bit more hands-off.

The Drop-In Polyfill

The next type of polyfill is the so-called *drop-in*, or *pure*, polyfill. I've chosen this name to indicate a polyfill that adheres to the API of the feature in question while requiring no additional configuration beyond a script include. When included, a drop-in polyfill goes to work by adding its functionality to the browser, typically via additions to Java-Script prototypes or globals such as `window` or `document`. Once the polyfill is included and parsed, the developer is free to rely on standard functionality without the need for additional feature detects or user agent interrogation.

Let's take a look at a simple, yet appropriate example: `String.trim()`. This useful function is included in all modern browsers, but is notably absent from IE6–8. If you're tasked with supporting these browsers, and you absolutely must trim your strings with a built-in function, you can add that needed functionality via a drop-in polyfill, as illustrated in Example 1-4, courtesy of Mozilla's excellent MDN documentation (*http://bit.ly/mdn-docu*).

Example 1-4. Creating a drop-in polyfill for `String.trim()`

```
if(!String.prototype.trim) {
  String.prototype.trim = function () {
    return this.replace(/^\s+|\s+$/g,'');
  };
}
```

In this example, we're checking to see whether the `trim` function exists on the `String` prototype, and if not, we add a new function that performs a simple RegEx replacement. To leverage this polyfill, a developer need only include it somewhere in her app before the first call to `trim`. If `trim` does indeed exist, our polyfill isn't needed and thus, nothing happens. It may seem like a minor point, but it's important to note that a good polyfill is aware of its execution environment and adds functionality only when needed. We'll talk more about this in the next chapter.

The biggest advantage of the drop-in polyfill is hands-off adoption for the developer. Because the workflow for using this type of library is a single step—include the library in your app—this type of approach is quite appealing for many developers looking for a quick solution that takes them out of the feature-detection game.

That said, the biggest benefit of the drop-in polyfill can also be a weakness. A drop-in polyfill can mislead developers into thinking that the API they are looking to leverage is both fully supported and implemented in a similar manner as standard approaches taken by already-supporting browsers. If your polyfill deviates from the spec in any way, or behaves unpredictably, you run the risk of confusing or annoying the developers who rely on your tool. As a result, building drop-in polyfills is not for the faint of heart. Taking on this type of library necessitates a deep understanding of the relevant spec, as well as some knowledge of the inner-workings of compliant implementations in other browsers.

It also requires that you either support the entire API of a given feature, or be crystal clear which aspects you do and don't support in your documentation. By definition, drop-in polyfills can be subdivided into two types: those that fully fill a complete feature API, and those that fill only a portion of that API. An example of the latter subtype is the excanvas polyfill (*http://bit.ly/xcanvas*), which supports much of the HTML5 Canvas API, but does not support the rendering of text via the standard `fillText` and `stroke Text` APIs. For text, the developer must either avoid using these functions, or leverage an additional polyfill for this functionality. While a partial drop-in polyfill is still useful, it somewhat obviates the benefits of building this type of library because the developer still must feature-test for those aspects of the API not supported by your library. It's not always possible or sensible to fully support a standard API, of course, but where possible, you should make every effort to do so when building this type of polyfill.

The Forward Polyfill

The last type of polyfill is an emerging type: the *prollyfill*. According to Alex Sexton, who coined the term, a prollyfill is "a polyfill for a not yet standardized API." These types of libraries, also called *forward polyfills*, are unique in that they are not designed to fill existing standards gaps, as polyfills have done traditionally. Rather, these polyfills are designed to test new or emerging standards inside browsers.

The prollyfill pattern is becoming more and more important to web developers and standards authors alike because they create a feedback loop between developers, spec authors, and browser engineers that's heretofore been unseen on the Web. Traditionally, browser standardization has been very top-down, and often developers have no opportunity to experiment with new APIs until these are implemented in one or more browsers. If you want proof that top-down standardization isn't always the best approach, see XHTML 2.0, Microformats, Web SQL, Application Cache, or any number of standards that failed to gain traction once subjected to real-world use by developers.

Prollyfills bring a bottom-up, democratized process to the open Web by allowing developers to experiment with and iterate on candidate APIs *before* they move into stable browser implementations. Prollyfills can also emerge from new libraries and languages that weren't formed with the goal of shaking up the world of web standards. Take CoffeeScript, for instance, as shown in Example 1-5:

Example 1-5. CoffeeScript's "dash rocket" and fat-arrow function syntax

```
square = (x) -> x * x
cube   = (x) => square(x) * x
```

Though CoffeeScript isn't really a prollyfill, it's a great example of how developer adoption of an idea can drive the standardization process, as evidenced by TC39's acceptance of fat-arrow function syntax into ECMAScript 6, as shown in Example 1-6:

Example 1-6. Arrow function syntax in ECMAScript 6

```
let square = x => x * x;
let cube = x => square(x) * x;
```

Prollyfills are an important concept, and they are a big reason for my writing this book. A deeper discussion of these, the rationale behind them, and various approaches for building prollyfills can be found in the latter half of this book. In the meantime, let's talk about why polyfills should and do still matter to web developers.

Why Polyfills Still Matter

In the current era of faster updates to browsers—including our favorite punching bag, Internet Explorer—it's easy to dismiss polyfills as a passing fad that have offered little more than to inform the early days of HTML5 adoption. In some ways, this claim isn't unfair. When polyfills first entered the developer consciousness, their goal was singular: easing the path to HTML5 adoption by reducing the amount of platform-specific code needed to leverage a new feature. Had the polyfilling pattern never grown beyond this scope, we probably wouldn't be talking about them much these days.

And yet, polyfills remain part of our everyday frontend vernacular. I believe this is for a couple of reasons. For starters, for HTML5 and beyond (the open Web, if you will), browser vendors continue to adopt emerging technologies at differing paces. While some browsers tend to add features as early as possible for the purpose of developer testing and feedback, others prefer to iterate solely in the standards bodies, adopting features only as they move further through the process and mature. It's outside the scope of this book and well beyond this author's temperament to render judgment on which of these approaches is more ideal, but these differences are worth mentioning because they point to the continued importance of polyfills. As long as browser x implements a different set of emerging features than browsers y or z, the need for polyfills remains.

Another reason for the continued importance of the polyfill is the emergence of the *prollyfill*, as described in the last section. The prollyfill variation has appeared over the last year in response to an ever-growing number of developers desiring to get involved earlier in the standards process. Prollyfills are a tool of choice for developers looking to "extend the Web forward." In the recent Extensible Web Manifesto, polyfills were described as the catalyst that aids in creating a "virtuous cycle" between web developers and the W3C's standardization process:

Making new features easy to understand and polyfill introduces a virtuous cycle:

- Developers can ramp up more quickly on new APIs, providing quicker feedback to the platform while the APIs are still the most malleable.

- Mistakes in APIs can be corrected quickly by the developers who use them, and library authors who serve them, providing high-fidelity, critical feedback to browser vendors and platform designers.

- Library authors can experiment with new APIs and create more cow-paths for the platform to pave.

— The Extensible Web Manifesto
http://extensiblewebmanifesto.org

Over the last few years, polyfills have grown from an HTML5 adoption tactic to a popular library development pattern and, finally, a full-blown standardization strategy. As a polyfill developer, you may be building your library with one of these targets in mind. Regardless of whether your polyfill is practical, tactical, or strategic in nature, you'll want to keep some guiding principles and practices in mind as you set out to build your library. We'll discuss these in the next chapter.

CHAPTER 2

Principles and Practices of Polyfill Development

In Chapter 1, we talked about what polyfills are and are not, various types of polyfills, and why these libraries are still important in the world of web development. In this chapter, I'm going to introduce the concept of *responsible polyfills*, that is, polyfills built to serve the needs of the consuming web developer. It's a common sense subject, for sure, but one that I still believe warrants explicit discussion.

Once I've introduced the *responsible polyfills* concept, I'll share some principles of poly-fill development to use as your guide, regardless of the type of library you're building. For many of these principles, the discussion will include some of the common challenges and pitfalls of polyfilling you might run into.

Building Responsible Polyfills

When building a polyfill, or any library for that matter, you'll probably start by asking yourself several questions. For instance:

- Why is this library necessary?
- Why am I building it?
- What should this library do?
- How will developers want to use it?

For most of us, the act of creating a new piece of software is driven by an unmet need of our own. If you encounter a platform feature not supported in all browsers, and think that you have the skills, time, and desire to create a polyfill, that may be all it takes to get you started. And, as the developer and first user of your library, you often have a good handle on answering most or all of the preceding questions.

Even still, if you're creating a library as open source or publicly available software, you're probably not doing it for yourself alone. You may be the first user, but you don't want to be the only one. As such, planning the creation of your polyfill should be an exercise in thinking about the variety of needs and contexts that developers will bring to the table when using your library.

I call this practice responsible polyfilling because it's not just for yourself and your needs, but for the needs of as many developers as possible. This means that you need to think about things like performance, the execution environment, and even planned obsolescence. Responsible polyfills are polyfills that don't make the developer pay a tax for using them, be that a performance tax, maintenance tax, or otherwise. Responsible polyfills give developers options based on their context and needs, and don't force them down a narrow path built solely for the library developer.

Responsible polyfilling is about having a clear purpose, clear goals and non-goals, and about following a couple of basic principles during development. We'll talk about principles in the next section, but the first and most important step in polyfill development is to define the purpose and goals for your library.

The Polyfill Vision Statement

Much like a vision statement for a new company or product, your polyfill needs something to clearly define why it exists, what benefit it provides, and what it will and won't offer to developers. This little bit of advance planning helps drive development and clearly communicates your values. It can also spur additional feedback from developers who might have different or expanded needs from your library, thereby allowing you to enhance your polyfill, if doing so makes sense.

All this vision statement babble might sound like a lot of work for an open source library, but it doesn't have to be. A half-hour spent defining what your polyfill is all about will streamline your development, keep you focused on the things that matter, and save you tons of time and headaches down the road.

Let's look at an example. In the next few chapters, I'm going to walk step-by-step through the construction of a polyfilling library that uses Kendo UI (*http://www.kendoui.com*) widgets to fill in the missing or inconsistent parts of the HTML5 Forms experience across all browsers, including IE7/8. When I started this project, I sat down and defined three things:

- The scope and vision for the library
- Its goals
- Its non-goals

This vision statement can be found on the home page for the project (*http://bit.ly/kendo-ui*), but I'll include it here so you can see an example of what I mean:

Purpose and Goals of the Kendo UI HTML5 Forms Polyfill

The purpose of this project is to serve as a complete polyfill for HTML5 Forms (*http://bit.ly/html5-forms*) functionality, including support for new input types (like `color` and `datetime`), new attributes (like `placeholder` and `pattern`), and validation. This project includes built-in feature detection and, by default, will polyfill only those forms features not present in the user's browser. To polyfill forms features, Kendo UI widgets and framework features will be used.

If developers prefer not to use the default behavior, they will be able to configure the polyfill to always use Kendo UI widgets and features, even in cases where the browser natively supports these.

This library will function as an opt-in polyfill, meaning that the developer will need to initialize a form using Kendo UI's imperative, plug-in syntax (e.g., `$("form").kendo Form();`) or with declarative syntax on an HTML form element (for example, `<form data-role="form">`).

Goals

- Provide a complete HTML5 Forms solution that leverages Kendo UI for visual widgets and features such as validation.

- Enable developers to mark up forms using HTML5 Forms semantics and automatically gain support for these in nonsupporting browsers. Anecdotally, in a future world where all browsers fully support the forms spec, a developer should be able to remove the script reference for this library and the single attribute or line of code that initializes it and have a nonbroken, fully functional experience.

- Ensure that performance is a feature. This library should tax the developer and end user as little as possible, making the benefit of use far higher than the cost of development, maintenance, or performance.

Non-Goals

- This library will not support configurable or drop-in replacement for another UI/widget library.

- This library will not diverge from the HTML5 Forms spec in order to add convenience features or nonstandard behaviors.

As you can see, in just a few hundred words, I'm able to clarify important features of the library, why it exists, and even spend some time being specific about what the library does and doesn't do. If I hadn't written this ahead of time, I might have missed important features or configuration options, or overlooked the importance of performance. I might have even taken on large, burdensome features—like swappable library support —without thinking them through ahead of time.

When you set out to build your polyfill, spend an hour or so thinking about some of those important Ws from journalism and composition: Who, What, Why, When, Where, and of course, How. The exercise will provide you with laser-like focus and set you up for success.

Speaking of success, let's build on our vision statement and talk about some principles for building responsible polyfills.

Principles of Responsible Polyfill Development

I'm a big fan of guiding principles and patterns, and not so much a fan of lists of rules. In my experience, it's too easy to allow lists of rules to turn into checklists and, when that happens, one can lose all sense of context around the current problem—meaning, rules tend to be rote, often applied without context. Principles, on the other hand, encourage the application of context because they force us to consider how to uniquely apply a given principle to the current problem. Sometimes a principle will be incorporated in a straightforward matter. In other scenarios, a given principle may not even apply to the problem at hand. Either way, it's up to the developer to decide, not the crafter of the principles themselves.

With that bit of soapboxing out of the way, let's talk about principles for responsible polyfill development. Remember that the goal of responsible polyfilling is to build for the needs of developers using your library. With that goal in mind, here are the six principles that I believe can help you build reliable polyfills for other developers:

- Read the spec
- Respect the API, if possible
- Mind (only) the gaps
- Think like a browser developer
- Build with performance in mind
- Plan for obsolescence

Let's talk about each of these in turn.

Read the Spec

I do a lot of reading. About half of my reading is technical (blog posts, articles, and books) and the other half is not; things like great novels and books about the joys and trials of raising three precocious boys. Across these, there are a lot of things I love to read, and many things that require a monumental force of will for me to power through.

Specifications, be they the W3C or WHATWG variety, fall squarely into that latter category. If I'm being completely honest, and in a private conversation with a close friend,

I'd probably even admit that I'd rather paint my living room, pull up a lawn chair, and watch that paint dry while licking 9-volt batteries, than willingly read a W3C specification.

This is not to say that these specifications aren't useful or even a worthwhile read. As a matter of fact, they are enormously useful to their primary audience: browser implementers. And they are worth your time as a polyfill developer. Much like my four-year-old needs to be reminded that eating vegetables is important, I have to be reminded from time to time that specifications are very useful, even to us lowly web developers.

For the polyfill developer, reading and understanding a specification is almost as important as it is to browser implementers themselves. As we'll discuss in the next principle, reading the spec is the best way to understand *what* your polyfill needs to provide and thus is essential. It's the most rule-like of all these principles, but also the most important. So pull up a chair, put on a pot of coffee, get yourself a Ludovico apparatus, and get to work.

Respect the API, If Possible

When reading W3C specifications, you'll often come across blocks of text and pseudocode, similar to those found in Figure 2-1. This code is called *Web IDL*, an interface definition language designed for browsers. According to its specification (*http://bit.ly/web-idl*), Web IDL "is an IDL variant with a number of features that allow the behavior of common script objects in the web platform to be specified more readily."

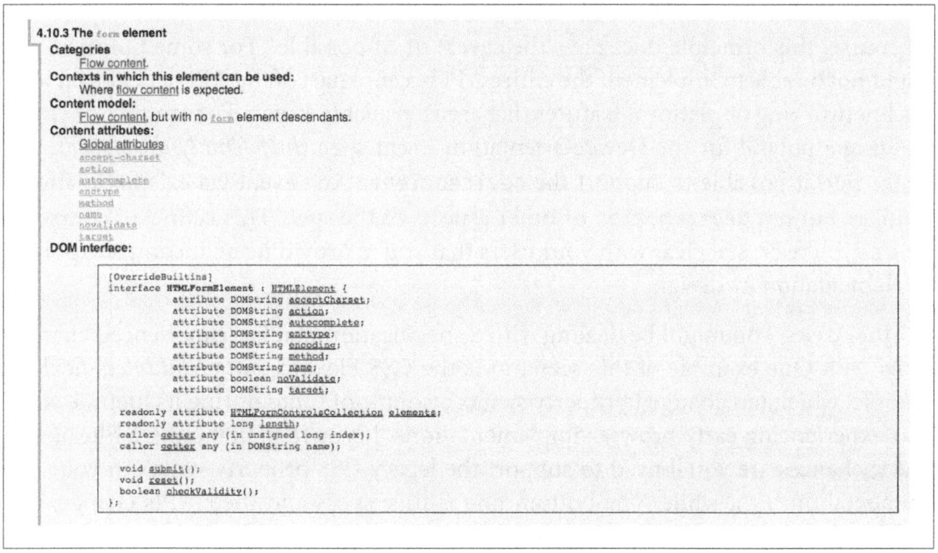

4.10.3 The form element

Categories
Flow content.
Contexts in which this element can be used:
Where flow content is expected.
Content model:
Flow content, but with no form element descendants.
Content attributes:
Global attributes
accept-charset
action
autocomplete
enctype
method
name
novalidate
target
DOM interface:

```
[OverrideBuiltins]
interface HTMLFormElement : HTMLElement {
           attribute DOMString acceptCharset;
           attribute DOMString action;
           attribute DOMString autocomplete;
           attribute DOMString enctype;
           attribute DOMString encoding;
           attribute DOMString method;
           attribute DOMString name;
           attribute boolean noValidate;
           attribute DOMString target;

  readonly attribute HTMLFormControlsCollection elements;
  readonly attribute long length;
  caller getter any (in unsigned long index);
  caller getter any (in DOMString name);

  void submit();
  void reset();
  boolean checkValidity();
};
```

Figure 2-1. Example WebIDL snippet for the HTML form element

So Web IDL specifies the interface that browsers are to use when building a standard implementation, and browsers do exactly that. What's more, most of them—perhaps even all of them, but I can't claim all without seeing Internet Explorer's code base, which is not open source—automatically generate Web IDL bindings directly from the spec-defined IDL. Chrome even includes Web IDL docs (*http://bit.ly/idl-blink*) for developers working with the browser source.

 While it's true that not all W3C specifications use Web IDL at present, the Web IDL spec itself was moved into Candidate Recommendation status in early 2012, so it's likely that the newer spec you're looking to polyfill will be written using this syntax.

There's no doubt that JavaScript API design is hard work. It's easy to get it wrong, and the chances of doing something you'll later regret are high. Because of this, one of the best parts of building polyfills is that your API is already defined for you! While W3C specs contain a lot of information you'll need to absorb for your polyfill, Web IDL is the icing on the cupcake, giving you the exact shape of your API, and all you need to do is make sense of it. What's more, with efforts like WebIDL.js (*http://bit.ly/webidl-js*) from the Extensible Web Community Group, getting a boilerplate API for your library might soon be as easy as running some IDL through the terminal.

The bottom line of this principle is that, most of the time, the API of your polyfill should be a pretty cut and dried effort. My advice is to extract the defined interfaces from the spec and make sure to implement those. No more, and no less.

Of course, this principle does have the caveat of "if possible." For some libraries, you might not be able to implement the entire API because part of the API depends on low-level networking or platform features that aren't available to you. For example, if you're building a polyfill for the DeviceOrientation Event spec (*http://bit.ly/devo-spec*), you might find it possible to support the `deviceorientation` event via existing platform features, but not `devicemotion` or other aspects of the spec. This is fine, of course, as long as you're crystal clear with your users that you're providing an incomplete polyfill implementation by design.

In other cases, you might be dealing with a specification that has experienced changes to its API. One example of this scenario is the CSS Flexbox (*http://bit.ly/css-flexbox*) module, which has changed property syntax a couple of times during its lifetime while also experiencing early browser implementations. If you're maintaining a Flexbox library, chances are you'll need to support the legacy CSS property syntax in your implementation for a while. The bottom line is this: specs and their APIs change, and building a polyfill might require you to bridge the gap created by API changes, in addition to merely filling in the gaps for browsers.

Mind (Only) the Gaps

This is a simple principle, but an important one to highlight nonetheless. When building your polyfill, it's important to never lose sight of the fact that your library's purpose in life is to fill in the gaps in other browsers—or to iterate on experimental APIs, in the case of a prollyfill—and nothing more. You should resist the temptation to add non-standard features simply because you want them or developers are clamoring for them. You can always create a separate shim that depends on your polyfill and add these features, but you'd be wise to keep them out of your main library.

Of course, prollyfills, which we'll discuss in Chapters 6 and 7, are an exception to this principle. Because the point of a prollyfill is to help vet an emerging API, you *should* experiment with new ideas and interfaces that you believe belong in the spec.

Think Like A Browser Developer

As I mentioned in the first principle, most W3C specifications are written by browser developers for browser developers. And while efforts like the Extensible Web movement are hoping to change that reality, for now, many of the specs in the standards pipeline were written by the people who will be adding those features to our browsers. I'm not going to weigh in here on whether that reality is or isn't an ideal world, but I do bring this point up to underscore an important fact: when you're building polyfills, you need to think like the C++ developer who is working on this feature in the browser. "Thinking like a browser developer" can take a number of forms:

- Following feature and spec discussions on the appropriate W3C Working Group mailing list.

- Following the implementation discussion in the issue trackers for Chrome (*http://bit.ly/chr-issues*) or Firefox (*http://bit.ly/fire-comp*). Google and Mozilla developers do a very good job of working in the open, so these trackers reveal a lot of insight into the various design decisions that go into implementing a given feature.

- Asking questions of developers on Internet Relay Chat (IRC). Picking a browser developer's brain via IRC can be one of the best ways to tap into implementation knowledge. It may sound daunting, but if you let these folks know that you're working on a polyfill for the feature they're working on, most will be happy to help. The Chrome team can be reached at #blink-dev on freenode, while Mozilla engineers typically hang out at #firefox on irc.mozilla.org. For more information on getting started with IRC, check out #irchelp (*http://www.irchelp.org/*).

Build With Performance in Mind

If you talk to web developers who have been working with HTML5 for a couple of years, you might discover that many hold the opinion that polyfills are nice, but too often, slow. Sometimes, when developers create a polyfill, they're interested first in covering features. Once those are delivered, the developers usually pack up their gear and head home, thinking the job is done.

But the truth is, performance is important when adopting HTML5 features, even when polyfilling older browsers. While your library cannot hope to match native browser performance, you should make every effort to make your library as fast as possible. After all, a poorly performing polyfill will end up being a bigger nightmare to end users —and thus developers—than if the developer just omitted the nonstandard feature in the first place.

There are a couple of ways you can build for performance. First, you can benchmark your implementation against native (i.e., the browser) using a tool like JSPerf (*http://jsperf.com*) and then iterate the heck out of your library until you can't iterate anymore. Second, you can create a robust set of unit tests with your polyfill, and make sure that these are tested using a cross-browser automated testing framework, like Karma (*http://bit.ly/karma-js*). We'll look at both of these strategies in Chapters 3 through 5.

Plan for Obsolescence

Polyfills, by their nature, are temporary. Unless you're building a shim with a brand new API—and thus, not a polyfill—your goal should never be to build the next jQuery or Backbone. As a polyfill developer, recognize that you're in the humbling business of building libraries that you *want* to become irrelevant in the future. The good news is that, for as long as developers need your library to fill in a key feature, it will be a welcome addition to their toolset. But we should never forget that the ultimate goal is to push for a world where these features exist native to all the browsers. It may seem that it goes without saying, but planning for obsolescence, along with complementary principles like "mind (only) the gaps," will help you stay focused on polyfilling and only polyfilling, while resisting the urge to morph your library into something that's part polyfill and part shim. A *phrankenfill*, if you will.

Take a look back at the principles for development, specifically the second bullet under "Goals." The second sentence indicates that a goal of my Kendo UI Forms polyfill is to allow the developer to remove the library in a fully compliant browser and not lose any functionality whatsoever. Not only does this keep me focused on the spec, and only the spec, but it is an example of planning for obsolescence.

A great example of planned obsolescence comes from the Apache Cordova/PhoneGap project. In a post entitled "PhoneGap Beliefs, Goals, and Philosophy," (*http://bit.ly/pg-goals*) Brian Leroux states that "the ultimate goal of the PhoneGap project is to cease to exist." He goes on to explain this seemingly defeatist statement as anything but:

Our second goal is not nihilistic but is rather a commitment to standardization of the Web as a platform. We believe in a Web open to everyone to participate however they will. No locked doors. No walls. The things we do with PhoneGap are directly influenced by the work we see at the W3C, WHATWG, and other research such as Mozilla's WebAPI, BONDI, WAC, webinos, webOS, Tizen, and the like.

Over the last five years, Apache Cordova (aka PhoneGap) has become the de facto wrapper for building hybrid mobile apps with HTML5. It would be easy for the founders and their benefactors to focus on sustaining this little kingdom of theirs. Instead, they point to the open Web as the reason they exist, as well as the reason they one day hope to shutter the project. It's an admirable attitude, and one we'd all be wise to emulate when building polyfills of our own.

Each of the preceding principles is designed to reinforce the goal of building responsible polyfills for developers. If you build your polyfill with some or all of these principles in mind, you'll go a long way toward delivering a robust, dependable, well-performing library that developers will love to use.

Now that we've talked about some of the key principles of building responsible polyfills, let's get to work. In the next chapter, I'll walk you through building a complete polyfill, step-by-step, using the principles found in this chapter.

CHAPTER 3

Building Your First Polyfill, Part 1: Getting Started

Over the last two chapters, we've covered why polyfilling is still important, as well as some principles for responsible polyfill development. In this chapter, I'm going to walk through some practical steps for building cross-browser polyfills via an actual, real-world project that I created. We won't go through every line of code or every excruciating detail, but I will introduce you to some practical examples and considerations that you'll want to keep in mind for your own polyfill development, no matter the web platform feature being targeted. We'll start with a discussion on project setup and structure before diving into setting up your API and deciding what you plan to build and not to build. Then we'll explore adding basic features and refactoring your polyfill as you expand scope over time. We'll then wrap up the chapter with a look at manual cross-browser testing, and some tips for streamlining your cross-browser testing workflow.

The HTML5 Forms Polyfill

First, let's take a look at our candidate library for the next two chapters: an HTML5 Forms polyfill. When I first set out to write this book, I considered a lot of different options for a guinea pig polyfill to use. I wanted to target something that was reasonably complex, but straightforward enough to introduce in bits and pieces, via text. I also wanted to choose a technology whose implementation status across browsers was more than just "supported in everything but IE." And even though IE will factor into some of the hairier aspects of our polyfill development, I wanted to walk through an example with quirks in as many browsers as possible. For those purposes, there's no better technology to attempt to polyfill than HTML5 Forms.

What we know of today as "HTML5 Forms" was actually the first technology to be proposed under the umbrella of what eventually became HTML5. First introduced outside the W3C as Web Forms 2.0 by a consortium of browser vendors that included

Google, Mozilla, Opera Software, and Apple, this proposal arrived at a time when the W3C was still pouring much of its effort into the now-defunct XHTML 2.0 specification. As an outflow of Web Forms 2.0, these vendors formed the Web Hypertext Application Technology Working Group (WHATWG), a sibling standards body to the W3C that still exists today.

And while it is outside of the scope of this book to discuss the politics of HTML5, various collected standards, and competing standards bodies, it is important to note that HTML5 Forms has not only been around a while, but it's still one of the most hotly debated aspects of the HTML5 spec. While certain aspects of the Forms spec have near universal support (for example, forms constraint validation), some of the more visual aspects of the spec (new input types like `number`, `color`, and `datetime`) have yet to be consistently implemented across all browsers, as illustrated in Figure 3-1. What's more, in some cases, for those browsers that do support certain types, the specifics of said support are often inconsistent from one implementation to the next. This means that you, the developer, might not get exactly the behavior you expect, every time, in every browser.

HTML5 Forms is a minefield, and I can't think of a better area in which to venture as a polyfill developer. It's a bit hairy, for sure, but this area of the spec is sufficiently complex enough to expose many of the polyfilling practices that I introduced in the preceding chapter.

In addition to targeting HTML5 Forms with my polyfill, I've chosen to leverage Kendo UI to provide much of the functionality that my polyfill will deliver to older browsers, from visual elements like color and date pickers, to key framework-level features like form validation. All of the UI widgets and framework features I need for my polyfill are available in the open source version of Kendo UI, which is available from its website (*http://www.kendoui.com*). That said, if you're following along and prefer to instead use a UI library like jQuery UI (*http://jqueryui.com*), you're welcome to do so. In fact, I've built a version of this polyfill using jQuery UI, and you can find it on GitHub (*http:// bit.ly/ui-forms*). Very little of what I cover in this chapter is dependent upon and applicable to only Kendo UI.

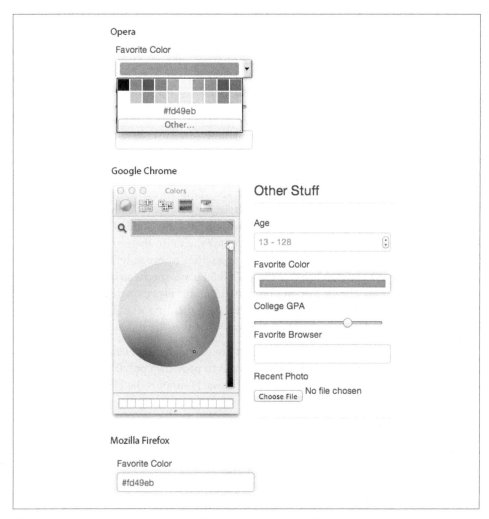

Figure 3-1. Color inputs viewed in Opera, Chrome, and Firefox

Why Use a Library?

At this point, you may be asking yourself why I've chosen to use a library like jQuery UI or Kendo UI at all. Why not just build the UI for each input type from scratch? It's a valid question, and in fact there are several great HTML5 Forms libraries out there that take this approach. If you're interested in taking a look at the code required to deliver UI widgets from scratch, I encourage you to check one of these out.

In our case, however, I've chosen to use a UI library because it allows me to focus on the process of building polyfills, which is, after all, what this book is about. By starting with a library that I can plug in, I'm able to focus on tips and tricks that are common to all types of polyfills, without getting bogged down in the very complex specifics of building form UI by hand.

 The HTML5 Forms polyfill we will be building over the next three chapters can be found in its current form online on GitHub (*http:// bit.ly/kendo-ui*). The project is actively maintained, and you're welcome to view the source after reading this book if you want to dig deeper into any specifics that I was unable to cover here.

Finally, it's worth mentioning that I've decided to build my HTML5 Forms polyfill as an opt-in polyfill, as opposed to a drop-in library. While it's certainly possible to do the latter, I think the former is a better approach, in my case, for a couple of reasons. For starters, since I'm using Kendo UI to power my widgets, and Kendo UI requires explicit widget initialization, I feel that it's appropriate for me to do the same with my polyfill and require that the developer activate the capabilities of my polyfill. I've also chosen to pursue an opt-in approach because the HTML5 Forms spec is so broad and complex that I'm not sure if my library will ever be able to support every single corner of the spec to the letter. By taking an opt-in approach, and documenting what I do and don't support, I can make sure that the developers know what they are buying into.

That said, even though my polyfill is opt-in, it doesn't mean that I can't future-proof my library. Just as with a drop-in polyfill, my goal is to provide a polyfill that can be easily removed (along with a line of code) when all browsers support the HTML5 Forms spec.

Setting Up Your Polyfill Project

Regardless of the technology you choose to target with your polyfill, the two most important choices that you can make early on are:

- Which source control solution you plan to use
- What your initial project structure will look like.

Sure, you can start with "Source Control by Dropbox" at the beginning and name your polyfill `mylib.js` if you're just itching to get started, but a little bit of foresight and planning is, in my opinion, just as important to polyfill development as the code you write. As such, I'll use the next few sections to talk about these early considerations.

Choosing a Source Control Solution

The first step is to think about how and where you'll want to host your code so that you've got a backup and full project history in case things go wrong so other developers can find, leverage, and contribute to your project. For the first part, you'll want to choose a source control solution that's open source and widely used. Two examples are Git (*http://git-scm.com/*) and Mercurial (*http://mercurial.selenic.com/*). These two systems have a similar command-line syntax for working with files and code repositories, so some developers will be comfortable working with either. That said, Git is far and away the most popular source control system in use today, so you'll reach a larger body of potential collaborators by choosing that system.

When paired with a solid code-sharing site, your source control solution also gives you a platform for making your polyfill available to the world. You can not only store your polyfill source and history in these sites, but also make that source and history available for others, which is hopefully your goal as a polyfill developer. Just as Git is the most popular source control option around today, GitHub (*https://github.com/*) is the most popular option for hosting and collaborating on all manner of Git-based open source software projects. Other options worth considering, if GitHub is not your cup of tea, are Bitbucket (*http://www.bitbucket.com/*), which allows you to host both Git and Mercurial projects, and Microsoft's CodePlex (*http://www.codeplex.com/*), which supports Mercurial projects only. For the examples in this book, I've chosen Git as my source control solution and GitHub for code sharing and distribution.

Setting Up the Initial Project Structure

Once I've chosen a source control solution, I'm ready to set up my project. I'll start by creating a new folder for my polyfill, called *kendo-ui-forms* in my usual development folder on my machine. Then, I'll open a terminal window in that directory and initialize a new GitHub repo by running the `git init` command. Once you've initialized your own local Git repository, you'll want to connect it to the remote repository that will be hosting your project online, which you can do by running the following command: `git remote add git@github.com:yourusername/your-project-name.git`. If you're not familiar with setting up a new remote repository, head over to GitHub, create a new repository for your project, and follow the on-screen instructions.

With that done, your local and remote repositories will be all set up, and it will be time to add some essential project files. Here's the basic project structure I recommend for most open source polyfills (assuming a view from the folder root):

dist/
    The minified and concatenated files you plan to distribute (the "binaries" for your polyfill).

lib/
    Any third party libraries that your polyfill depends on (jQuery, Underscore).

sample/
    Sample and example code for the polyfill.

spec/
    Home for your unit tests, which we'll discuss in Chapter 4.

src/[js,css]

Source JavaScript and CSS files.

gitignore

A list of files for Git to ignore when found in your project. GitHub can create one of these files for you when creating a new project. If you go that route, select the Node template.

CHANGELOG.md

A laundry list of minor and breaking changes for each version of your library.

CONTRIBUTING.md

Essential if you plan to accept contributions for your project.

README.md

The readme file for your project. GitHub automatically treats this file as the main entry point when anyone visits your project. It should describe the purpose and goals of the polyfill—as I discussed in Chapter 1—features of the project, a road map for the project, installation and usage instructions, and anything else you think might be useful to consumers of or collaborators on your polyfill.

LICENSE.md

Every open source project needs a license. Which license you choose is up to you, but permissive licenses, such as MIT and Apache 2.0, will garner more interest and, possibly, participation from other developers. GitHub can also generate this file for you, based on the license chosen at project creation.

 Though I did take the LSAT once upon a time, please note that I am not an attorney, nor do I play one on the Internet. As such, my opinions on licensing should not be confused for legal expertise. Your best bet is to consult with a legal expert before choosing an open source license. You can also visit Choose A License (*http://chooseali cense.com/*) for more information about the dizzying array of open source licenses available. But still, you should talk to a lawyer if you want an expert legal perspective.

Specifying the API

Once your polyfill project is set up, your next important decision is determining how other developers will "call" your polyfill, if at all. As you'll recall, two of the important subtypes of polyfills are the opt-in and drop-in types. If you're building a drop-in polyfill, that essentially means that developers need only include a reference to your library in their projects. When your script is loaded, it automatically activates and goes to work. For these types of polyfills, the API of your library is straightforward and should match the API of the specified functionality you're emulating as much as possible.

If, on the other hand, you're building an opt-in polyfill, you'll need to provide some mechanism for developers to activate your library. How you choose to expose your polyfill to developers is up to you, but I recommend considering your audience, specifically what they are likely to expect and be comfortable with, as you design your API. For examples of how other libraries expose their opt-in APIs, you can check out examples on the Modernizr Polyfill List (*http://bit.ly/mod-list*). Since the HTML5 Forms polyfill I'm building will leverage Kendo UI, I've chosen to build my polyfill as a custom Kendo UI widget. By doing so, I can use Kendo UI's ready-made options for initializing my library. As a result, I gain an initialization API for my polyfill that's easy to use and familiar to developers, especially those already familiar with Kendo UI.

Initializing an Opt-In Polyfill

Kendo UI allows developers to initialize widgets in one of two ways. I can use jQuery-style widget initialization, as illustrated in Example 3-1, or I can use a declarative-style declaration, which hinges on placing `data-role` attributes on relevant elements in my markup. This approach is illustrated in Example 3-2. Note that the next few examples assume the inclusion of jQuery, Kendo UI JavaScript, and Kendo UI CSS in the page.

Example 3-1. Initializing my Forms polyfill using JavaScript

```
<form id="myForm">
  <!-- Rest of form declaration -->
</form>
<script>
  $('#myForm').kendoForm();
</script>
```

Example 3-2. Initializing my Forms polyfill via declarative initialization

```
<form action="input.html" data-role="form">
  <!-- Rest of form declaration -->
</form>
<script>
  kendo.init(document.body);
</script>
```

To support both of these approaches in my polyfill, I'll need to follow Kendo UI's recommended approach for creating custom widgets. First, I'll create the core source file for my polyfill in the *src/* folder for my project. I'll call it *kendo.forms.js*, which follows a naming convention similar to other Kendo UI source files. Then, in my new source file, I'll include the code in Example 3-3.

Example 3-3. Initial skeleton for the Kendo UI Forms polyfill

```
(function($, kendo) {
  var ui = kendo.ui,
    Widget = ui.Widget;
```

```
var Form = Widget.extend({
  init: function(element, options) {
    // base call to widget initialization
    Widget.fn.init.call(this, element, options);
  },
  options: {
    // the name is what will appear in the kendo namespace (kendo.ui.Form).
    // The jQuery plug-in would be jQuery.fn.kendoForm.
    name: 'Form'
  }
});

  ui.plugin(Form);
} (jQuery, kendo));
```

As illustrated here, my polyfill starts with an Immediately-Invoked Function Expression (*http://bit.ly/i-ife*) (IIFE) that specifies my dependencies (jQuery and Kendo UI in this case). Next, I create some local lookup variables to cache key parts of the Kendo UI namespace. Then, I create a new Form variable by calling the kendo.ui.Widget.ex tend() method, which takes care of handling the initialization types I specified. Finally, I'll call the kendo.ui.plugin() method and pass in my Form widget, which adds my polyfill to the widget registry for runtime lookup and evaluation.

For my HTML5 Forms polyfill, this is all I need to create a public API for initializing my library. With this skeleton code in place, I can now use either initialization method described in Example 3-1 and Example 3-2, and things will resolve. My polyfill won't do anything at this point, but it will run without errors, so that's progress!

With the opt-in API of our library set, we can move on to building out the core functionality of our polyfill. Regardless of the type of polyfill you're building, much of the API you'll be exposing should already be decided for you via the specification for the technology you're targeting. As discussed in the preceding chapter, it's important to adhere to this specification as much as possible. If you're planning to support an aspect of the spec, you should try your best to support it *as specced*. You should also be clear in your documentation and in-source comments about which aspects of the spec you support and which you don't.

Deciding What to Build

Speaking of which, the next important decision you need to make in your library is what to build. Even if you do plan to support every nook and cranny of a spec with your polyfill, you probably won't be able to bang out full support over a weekend. You need a plan, and if you're anything like me, you probably want to target simple features and "quick wins" first. This establishes a good foundation and a working polyfill before you tackle the hairier aspects of support. If you'd rather target the hard stuff, that's OK too!

In the context of HTML5 Forms, the simpler features are those new input types like color, number, and datetime. Because Kendo UI Web has widgets for these, supporting them is a simple matter of adding the Kendo UI widget when one of these types is found on a form. Validation support, on the other hand, is a bit trickier, so I'm going to put that off for later, perhaps after the first couple of releases.

Speaking of releases, this is probably a good time to think about the road map for your polyfill. Assuming you're talking about a complex feature, you'll probably want to write down what you plan to support, and when. For the HTML5 Forms polyfill, I chose to include a road map in the *readme* for the project, which I've also included in Table 3-1.

Table 3-1. Road map for the Kendo UI Forms polyfill

Release	Features
v0.1	Support upgrading all HTML5 input types (color, numeric, range, file, datetime, time, month, week).
v0.1.1	Button support and date type support.
v0.2	Add support for progress and datalist elements; add a placeholder fallback and search box UI; autocomplete attribute support.
v0.3	Add validation support.

In addition to creating a road map and plan for your polyfill, you'll want to consider whether there's anything under the technology umbrella of your polyfill that you don't plan to or cannot support. Sometimes it's not possible to reliably polyfill an aspect of a specification, so you'll want to avoid even trying to support it. Other times, adding support for a given feature is possible, but not something you're prepared to take on. No matter the reason, be sure that your road map is clear about what you're not planning to polyfill so that developers are informed when considering your library.

Adding Basic Features

So we've got our basic polyfill skeleton in place, an API for calling it, and a road map for which features we plan to add. Now it's time to get to work and add our first, real feature. Of course, if we're going to add features to our polyfill, we also need ways to test them out, don't we? In Chapter 4, I'll discuss setting up unit and cross-browser testing in depth, but in the meantime, let's create a sample form that we can use to test out our library as we work on it. This sample will serve as a live demonstration and part of our docs when we publish our polyfill, so it's something you'll want to add to your projects even if you're also performing automated testing. Consider it a way to show off all your hard work to your potential users.

Creating a Sample Form

To that end, let's create a new HTML page in the *samples/* folder and call it *form.html*. Since our library is an HTML5 Forms polyfill, it makes sense that the sample page itself contain a form showing off all of our bells and whistles. Since this sample page will also serve as a part of my docs, the HTML page, which you can view in the online repo for this project (*http://bit.ly/kendo-ui*), will include references to bootstrap and some additional markup that I've not included in Example 3-4. The relevant portion of this sample page, the form itself, is shown in Table 3-1.

Example 3-4. Sample markup for the Forms polyfill

```
<form action="#" id="sampleForm">
  <fieldset>
    <legend>Essentials</legend>
    <div>
      <label for="name">Name</label>
      <input type="text" required placeholder="ex. Hugo Reyes" />
    </div>
    <div>
      <label for="email">Email</label>
      <input type="email" required placeholder="ex. hugo@dharma.com" />
    </div>
    <div>
      <label for="phone">Phone</label>
      <input type="tel" placeholder="ex. 555-555-5555"
             pattern="^[2-9]\d{2}-\d{3}-\d{4}$"
             title="Use a XXX-XXX-XXXX format" />
    </div>
    <div>
      <label for="phone">Gratuitous Search</label>
      <input type="search" id="search" />
    </div>
  </fieldset>
  <fieldset>
    <legend>Dates and Times</legend>
    <div>
      <label for="birthday">Birthday</label>
      <input type="date" />
    </div>
    <div>
      <label for="doctor">Next Doctor's Appointment</label>
      <input type="datetime-local" value="2012-12-14T19:00"/>
    </div>
    <div>
      <label for="favMonth">What month is it?</label>
      <input type="month" />
    </div>
    <div>
      <label for="favMonth">When is Shark Week?</label>
      <input type="week" />
    </div>
    <div>
      <label for="favMonth">What time is Beer O'Clock?</label>
      <input type="time" />
    </div>
```

```
    </fieldset>
    <fieldset>
      <legend>Other Stuff</legend>
      <div>
        <label for="age">Age</label>
        <input type="number" min=13 max=128 required placeholder="13 - 128" />
      </div>
      <div>
        <label for="color">Favorite Color</label>
        <input type="color" value="#fd49eb" />
      </div>
      <div>
        <label for="GPA">College GPA</label>
        <input type="range" min=0.0 max=4.0 value=3.0 step=0.25 />
        <span id="rangeValue"></span>
      </div>
      <div>
        <label for="browser">Favorite Browser</label>
        <input type="text" list="browsers" />
        <datalist id="browsers">
          <option value="Chrome">
          <option value="Firefox">
          <option value="Internet Explorer">
          <option value="Opera">
          <option value="Safari">
        </datalist>
      </div>
      <div>
        <label for="picture">Recent Photo</label>
        <input type="file" />
      </div>
    </fieldset>
    <hr />
    <div>
      <div>Progress
        <progress id="completionPct" min=1 max=12 value=3></progress>
      </div>
      <br />
      <input type="submit" value="Submit this mess!" />
      <input type="submit" formnovalidate value="Save for later" />
    </div>
</form>
```

As you can see from the sample, it's a pretty robust form, and it also uses all of the new
HTML5 Forms features introduced in the spec, like new input types (such as color and
datetime), new attributes (like autocomplete, pattern, or required) and form validation features. To give you an idea of what this form looks like in various browsers,
Figure 3-2 shows what our form looks like, by default, in Chrome 29, while Figure 3-3
shows what the form looks like in Safari 6.1. Notice the difference in the date fields, the

favorite color field, and others. We've certainly got our work cut out for us with this polyfill, even without taking oldIE into account!

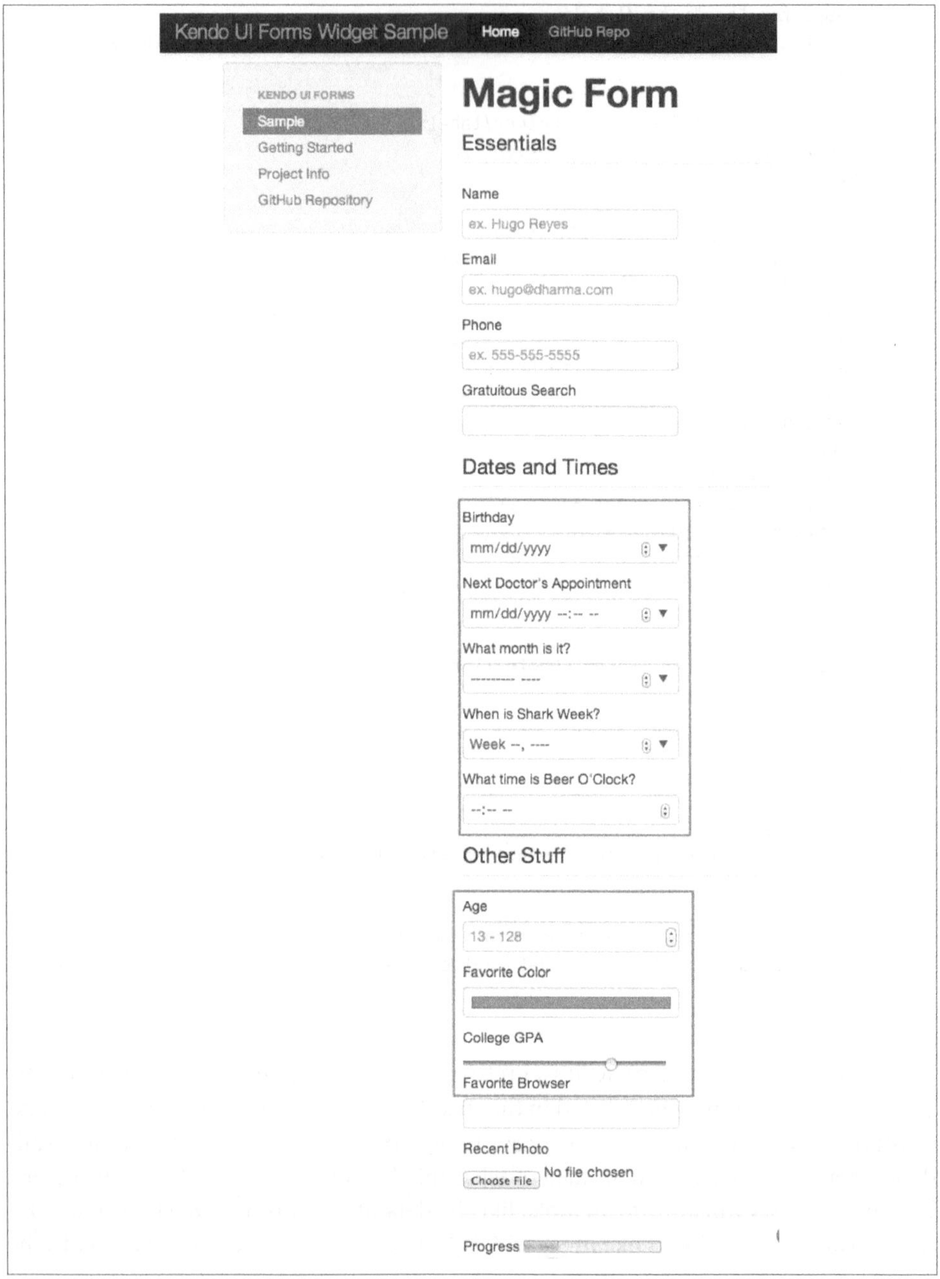

Figure 3-2. Sample form as viewed in Google Chrome 29

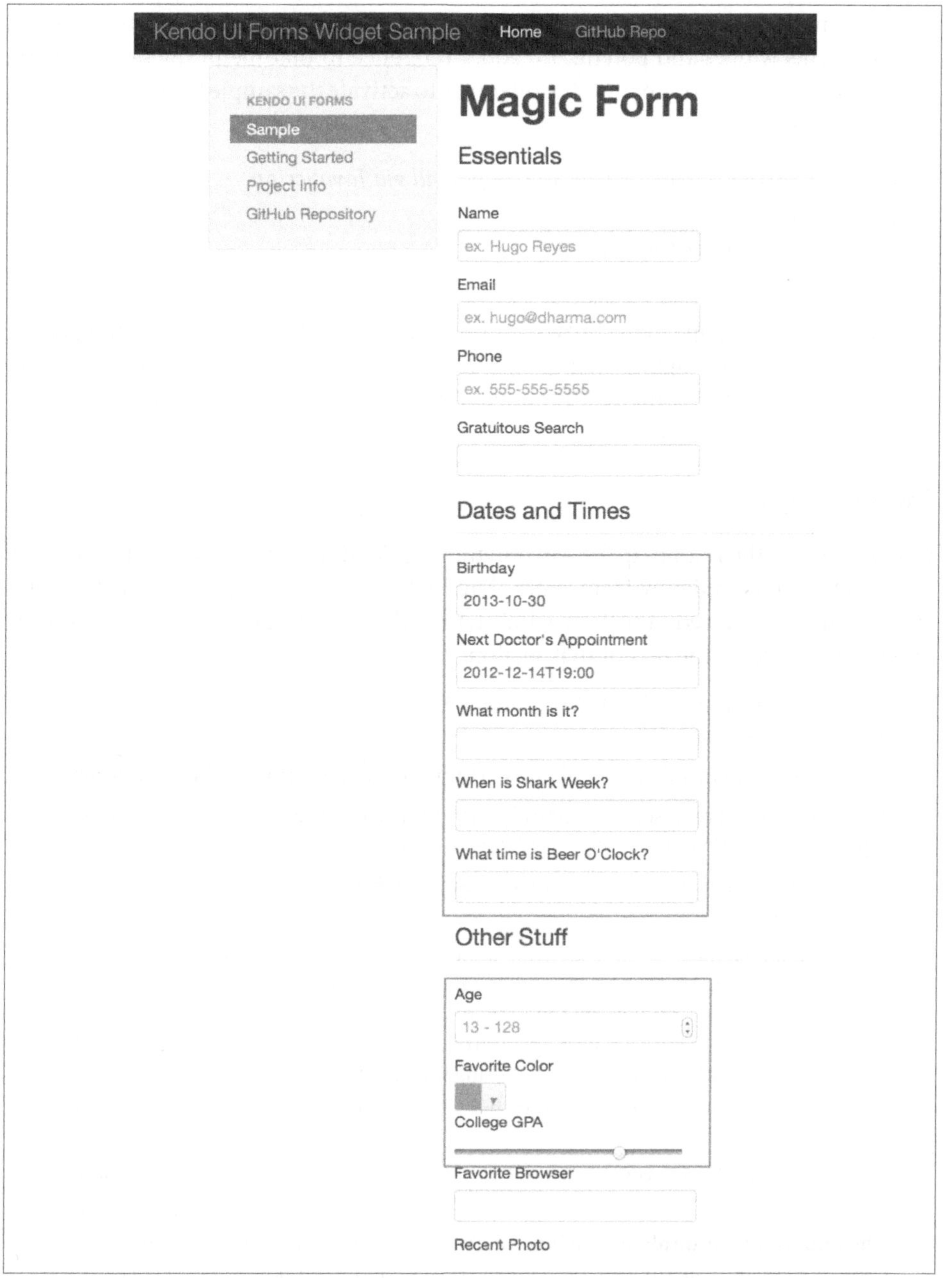
Kendo UI Forms Widget Sample
Home
GitHub Repo
KENDO UI FORMS
Sample
Getting Started
Project Info
GitHub Repository
Magic Form
Essentials
Name
ex. Hugo Reyes
Email
ex. hugo@dharma.com
Phone
ex. 555-555-5555
Gratuitous Search
Dates and Times
Birthday
2013-10-30
Next Doctor's Appointment
2012-12-14T19:00
What month is it?
When is Shark Week?
What time is Beer O'Clock?
Other Stuff
Age
13 - 128
Favorite Color
College GPA
Favorite Browser
Recent Photo

Figure 3-3. Sample form as viewed in Safari 6.1

With my sample form in place, I'll next need to add a reference to my polyfill source file. In Example 3-3, we created the main *kendo.forms.js* file, which included the skeleton for our Forms widget and polyfill. I'll add a reference to that file in my sample form, and then add a script block or new file reference to activate the sample form, as illustrated in Example 3-5.

Example 3-5. Activating our Forms opt-in polyfill via JavaScript

```
(function($, kendo) {
  $('#sampleForm').kendoForm();
}(jQuery, kendo));
```

Now, if I refresh the page in my browser, I'll see that nothing is different. I'm not getting any console errors, though, which means that my polyfill is being properly initialized. All that's left is to add some real functionality. So, without further ado, let's add that much-anticipated first feature.

Color Support

When I created the road map for my polyfill, I decided to tackle new input types first, and build up in complexity from there. The first type I'll add support for is the color option, which is covered in section 4.10.7.1.15 of the HTML5 Forms spec (*http://bit.ly/ numberstate*). Here's the text of that section:

> Color State Section of the HTML5 Forms Spec
> **4.10.7.1.15 Color state**
>
> When an input element's type attribute is in the Color state, the rules in this section apply.
>
> The input element represents a *color well control*, for setting the element's value to a string representing a simple color (*http://bit.ly/microsyntaxes*).
>
> *Note: In this state, there is always a color picked, and there is no way to set the value to the empty string.*
>
> If the element is mutable, the user agent should allow the user to change the color represented by its value, as obtained from applying the rules for parsing simple color values to it. User agents must not allow the user to set the value to a string that is not a valid lowercase simple color. If the user agent provides a user interface for selecting a color, then the value must be set to the result of using the rules for serializing simple color values to the user's selection. User agents must not allow the user to set the value to the empty string.
>
> The value attribute, if specified and not empty, must have a value that is a valid simple color.
>
> **The value sanitization algorithm is as follows**: If the value of the element is a valid simple color, then set it to the value of the element converted to ASCII lowercase; otherwise, set it to the string "#000000".
>
> **Bookkeeping details**

- The following common input element content attributes, IDL attributes, and methods apply to the element: autocomplete and list content attributes; list, value, and selectedOption IDL attributes.

- The value IDL attribute is in mode value.

- The input and change events apply.

- The following content attributes must not be specified and do not apply to the element: accept, alt, checked, dirname, formaction, formenctype, formmethod, formnovalidate, formtarget, height, maxlength, max, min, multiple, pattern, placeholder, readonly, required, size, src, step, and width.

- The following IDL attributes and methods do not apply to the element: checked, files, selectionStart, selectionEnd, selectionDirection, valueAsDate, and valueAsNumber IDL attributes; select(), setSelectionRange(), stepDown(), and stepUp() methods.

As noted in the preceding text, the "Color" type is intended to offer a simple "color well" control that supports visual selection of simple colors and retrieval of sRGB or hexadecimal equivalents of these. There's a lot of W3C-speak in the section, but the rules for implementing a color input type in a browser are pretty straightforward:

- The value attribute of an input with a type of `color` is a seven character string (# and six characters for the color value) that represents a valid sRGB color.

- A valid color value must always be selected; null and empty string values are not permitted.

- The default color value string is `#000000`, or black.

- The UI for the color type must be a mask input—that is, it will not accept values that do not represent a valid sRGB color.

- The string value for the color input should always be represented by a lowercase string, and converted to a lowercase string upon input, if uppercase characters are used.

You can see in Figure 3-2 that Chrome supports this attribute, while Safari 6.1 does not, as shown in Figure 3-3 (Safari simply shows the hex value I set in the sample form). Coincidentally, Kendo UI Web provides a `ColorPicker` (*http://bit.ly/k-colorpicker*) widget that follows all of the preceding rules, so this control is a great first addition to our polyfill.

When I initialize my polyfill by calling `kendoForm()` (or via the declarative approach), the `init()` method in Example 3-3 will be fired, so that's the right place to start adding my functionality. Inside that method, and just after the call to `Widget.fn.init`, I can add my color type code, as illustrated in Example 3-6.

Example 3-6. Adding color type support to the Forms polyfill

```
(function($, kendo) {
  var ui = kendo.ui,
    Widget = ui.Widget;

  var Form = Widget.extend({
    init: function(element, options) {
      // base call to widget initialization
      Widget.fn.init.call(this, element, options);

      var form = $(element);
      **`form.find('input[type=color]').kendoColorPicker({ palette: 'basic' });`**
    },
    options: {
      // the name is what will appear in the kendo namespace (kendo.ui.Form).
      // The jQuery plug-in would be jQuery.fn.kendoForm.
      name: 'Form'
    }
  });

  ui.plugin(Form);
} (jQuery, kendo));
```

In this sample, I'm looking for every input on my form with the attribute `type=color` and initializing a `kendoColorPicker` for each, using the `basic` palette option. The HTML5 specification doesn't have anything to say about what the color control should look like or how it should behave, visually, so I've chosen a sensible default for the `ColorPicker`. Now, when I view the sample form in Safari, Firefox, or Internet Explorer (all browsers that do not support the `color` type at the time of writing), I'll see a Kendo UI ColorPicker in place of the default text input, as seen in Figure 3-4.

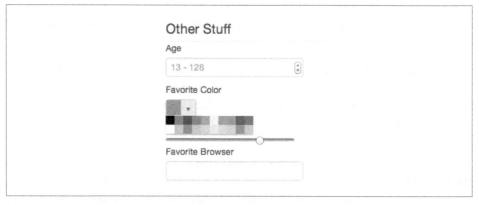

Figure 3-4. Color support in the Forms polyfill (Safari 6.1)

To Feature Detect or Not to Feature Detect

Of course, there's a catch. As it happens, if you view the sample page in a browser that *does* support the color type (like Chrome or Opera), you'll notice that a ColorPicker was created in these browsers as well. This is because my current implementation doesn't bother to perform feature detection for the color type, instead overriding every occurrence of the type on every browser.

 Feature detection is the practice of executing code in the browser for the purpose of determining whether that browser supports a given feature. The practice is considered superior to the classical practice of *browser* or *user-agent sniffing* because, rather than making wholesale decisions about which features to provide based on the user's browser, you can enable or disable functionality at the feature level, based on support, regardless of the browser in use.

When building a cross-browser polyfill, you'll need to consider how you wish to approach feature detection for your library. You have two choices:

1. Require that the user perform feature detection before including or opting in to your polyfill.
2. Perform feature detection on behalf of (or in addition to) the user.

The first approach is common for polyfills that cover a limited feature-set, or those that are activated on a per element or frequent basis. As Modernizr (*http://modern izr.com*) is widely used by developers, it's common to see polyfills used in a manner similar to Example 1-3. In this example, I'm using Modernizr to query for CSS border-radius support and, if it's not available in the user's browser, I'll opt in to PIE for a given set of elements.

When building polyfills that are a bit more expansive, or even more "intrusive" in the functionality they provide, I recommend performing feature detection on the developer's behalf. In the case of HTML5 Forms, my polyfill is instantiated at the form level, so asking the user to perform feature detection before calling my library would be an all-or-nothing proposition that would lead to my library being used for all HTML5 Forms features, or none of them at all. Instead, I'd rather provide the ability for the polyfill to selectively upgrade only those features *not* supported in the browser.

To check for support for the color input type, I'll create a function inside my init function to test for support for individual form types, as shown in Example 3-7:

Example 3-7. Testing for input type support

```
function isFormTypeSupported(type) {
  if (type === 'text') { return true; }
```

```
  var input = document.createElement('input');
  input.setAttribute('type', type);
  return input.type !== 'text';
}
```

First, I'll create an in-memory input element. Then I'll set its type attribute to the type variable provided by the caller. Finally, I'll check the type attribute. If its value is still text even after I set it to another value, such as color, that means that the browser does *not* support this input type. As such, I'll return false. If the value is retained, browser support is available, and I'll return true.

To leverage this home grown feature-detection method, I'll modify the code in Example 3-6 to first check for support, as shown in Example 3-8. Now if I refresh Chrome or Opera, the built-in browser support is back, while custom widget support provided by my polyfill will be leveraged for all other browsers.

Example 3-8. Checking for color type support before adding a ColorPicker widget

```
if (!isFormTypeSupported('color')) {
  form.find('input[type=color]').kendoColorPicker({ palette: 'basic' });
}
```

Adding Opt-In Overrides to Your Polyfill

Once I add feature detection to my polyfill, the color type will be "upgraded" only when the browser doesn't support this type. This is excellent for a default behavior, but what if the developer *wants* to author HTML5 Forms markup and have all of their form fields upgraded to widgets, regardless of browser support? This is obviously a case that falls outside specified HTML5 Forms behavior, but it's a feature I've chosen to add in my forms polyfill, for two reasons:

- With an opt-in polyfill, allowing developers to pass in options is easy.
- Since the visual aspects of HTML5 forms vary greatly from one browser to the next, even between browsers that support a new type, some developers may prefer the ability to author HTML5 Forms markup while gaining a consistent look and feel for visual widgets across browsers. It's downright "prollyfill-esque," but we'll get to that.

If you recall that one of our "responsible polyfilling" principles in Chapter 2 is "mind (only) the gaps," you probably think I'm contradicting myself right now by adding override capabilities to my library. And while an argument can be made for leaving out a feature such as this, I believe that it's a feature that adds value to the developer and end user by providing the ability to apply a consistent form UI across browsers. As such, I think it's appropriate. What's more, since the feature I'm adding doesn't "break" the end-user experience on supporting browsers if the polyfill is removed—it merely changes the look and feel of HTML5 Forms fields—I don't see it as a violation of the principle. Bottom line: These are principles, not rules. As the polyfill developer, you get to decide which ones to follow and which to discard, with good reason. If consumers of your library don't agree, they'll let you know.

To add an override for visual elements to my polyfill, I can leverage the built-in op tions object required by all Kendo UI widgets. In Example 3-3, we used this object to specify the name of our widget, Form, which Kendo UI uses when adding our polyfill to the library namespace. I can use this object to specify any number of developer-defined features, and I'll use it now to add an alwaysUseWidgets Boolean value. Once I've added that option, I'll modify my isFormTypeSupported method to check for this property. If alwaysUseWidgets is true, I'll skip the feature-detection test and return false. The full listing for our polyfill source, including color type support and the override, is shown in Example 3-9.

Example 3-9. Polyfill source with color type support and an alwaysUseWidgets option

```
(function($, kendo) {
  var ui = kendo.ui,
    Widget = ui.Widget;

  var Form = Widget.extend({
    init: function(element, options) {
      var form = $(element),
          that = this;

      // base call to widget initialization
      Widget.fn.init.call(this, element, options);

      function isFormTypeSupported(type) {
        if (type === 'text') { return true; }

        if (that.options.alwaysUseWidgets) { ❶
          return false;
        }

        var input = document.createElement('input');
        input.setAttribute('type', type);
        return input.type !== 'text';
      }

      if (!isFormTypeSupported('color')) {
        form.find('input[type=color]').kendoColorPicker({ palette: 'basic' });
      }
    },
    options: {
      // the name is what will appear in the kendo namespace (kendo.ui.Form).
      // The jQuery plug-in would be jQuery.fn.kendoForm.
      name: 'Form',
      alwaysUseWidgets: false ❷
```

```
    }
});

  ui.plugin(Form);
} (jQuery, kendo));
```

❶ Test the override property to determine if the element should always be upgraded

❷ Specify the override property and set the default value to false

With this functionality in place, I can modify my initialization code to pass in the `alwaysUseWidgets` option:

```
$('#sampleForm').kendoForm({ alwaysUseWidgets: true });
```

Now, the Kendo UI ColorPicker widget will be used in all browsers.

Beefing Up Your Polyfill with Additional Features

So far, we've added basic support for the `color` input type, feature detection for that type, and the ability to override detection and always upgrade the type to use a UI widget. And while it's nice to have support for a single type, it doesn't make for a terribly useful polyfill. Let's expand our polyfill by adding support for an additional input type.

Adding Support for the Number Type

The next feature for which I'll add support in my polyfill is the `number` input type, which is covered in section 4.10.7.1.13 of the HTML5 Forms specification (*http://bit.ly/ranges tate*):

Number State Section of the HTML5 Forms Spec
4.10.7.1.13 Number state

When an input element's type attribute is in the **Number** state, the rules in this section apply.

The input element represents a control for setting the element's value to a string representing a number.

If the element is mutable, the user agent should allow the user to change the number represented by its value, as obtained from applying the rules for parsing floating-point number values to it. User agents must not allow the user to set the value to a nonempty string that is not a valid floating-point number. If the user agent provides a user interface for selecting a number, then the value must be set to the best representation of the number representing the user's selection as a floating-point number. User agents should allow the user to set the value to the empty string.

The value attribute, if specified and not empty, must have a value that is a valid floating-point number.

The value sanitization algorithm is as follows: If the value of the element is not a valid floating-point number, then set it to the empty string instead.

The min attribute, if specified, must have a value that is a valid floating-point number. The max attribute, if specified, must have a value that is a valid floating-point number.

The step scale factor is 1. The default step is 1 (allowing only integers, unless the min attribute has a noninteger value).

When the element is suffering from a step mismatch, the user agent may round the element's value to the nearest number for which the element would not suffer from a step mismatch. If there are two such numbers, user agents are encouraged to pick the one nearest positive infinity.

The algorithm to convert a string to a number, given a string input, is as follows: If applying the rules for parsing floating-point number values to input results in an error, then return an error; otherwise, return the resulting number.

The algorithm to convert a number to a string, given a number input, is as follows: Return a valid floating-point number that represents input.

Bookkeeping details

- The following common input element content attributes, IDL attributes, and methods apply to the element: autocomplete, list, max, min, readonly, required, and step content attributes; list, value, valueAsNumber, and selectedOption IDL attributes; stepDown() and stepUp() methods.

- The value IDL attribute is in mode value.

- The input and change events apply.

- The following content attributes must not be specified and do not apply to the element: accept, alt, checked, dirname, formaction, formenctype, formmethod, formnovalidate, formtarget, height, maxlength, multiple, pattern, placeholder, size, src, and width.

- The following IDL attributes and methods do not apply to the element: checked, files, selectionStart, selectionEnd, selectionDirection, and valueAsDate IDL attributes; select() and setSelectionRange() methods.

As detailed in the spec, the number type is basically an edit mask that ensures that a user enters only numeric values into fields given the type="number" attribute value. Let's take the preceding wall of text and translate it into some simple rules:

- The value attribute of an input with a type of number is a floating-point number.

- A valid number value is *not* required at all times. If a valid number is not selected, the value is empty string.

- If the user attempts to enter an invalid or non-numeric value, the input value should be set to empty string.

- The min and max attributes are allowed on this input, and should both represent valid floating-point numbers.

- The `step` attribute is allowed and has a default value of 1, which allows only integers to be specified.
- If the value of the input is set programmatically and that value violates the specified `step` property (i.e., step is 1 and a value of 2.88 is set), the control should round the set value up or down based on rounding rules (in this example, the value would be set to 3).

Just as with the `color` type, Kendo UI Web has a NumericTestBox (*http://bit.ly/numer icbox*) widget that functions as a nice edit mask control for floating-point values, so we'll use this widget to polyfill nonsupporting browsers. Example 3-10 contains the code specific to `number` that I'll add to *kendo.forms.js*, just after my `color` type code.

Example 3-10. Adding number input type support to my Forms polyfill

```
if (!isFormTypeSupported('number')) {
  form.find('input[type=number]').kendoNumericTextBox();
}
```

To test this feature, I can load my sample form in a browser that doesn't support the `number` type, like IE9 or Firefox, or use the `alwaysUseWidgets` option. It works like a charm, and you'll also notice that attributes like `min` and `max`, which I specified for the Age field on my sample form in Example 3-4, were preserved by the Kendo UI Numer-icTextBox widget. I get that for free, which is awesome.

Even still, I can't help but get this creeping feeling that things could be better. To see what I mean, let's look at our two features together in Example 3-11:

Example 3-11. Color and number type support

```
if (!isFormTypeSupported('color')) {
  form.find('input[type=color]').kendoColorPicker({ palette: 'basic' });
}

if (!isFormTypeSupported('number')) {
  form.find('input[type=number]').kendoNumericTextBox();
}
```

Repetition everywhere! And while it doesn't look terrible with only two features, I can't even bear the thought of what my polyfill will look like once I add support for all of the 12+ visual types and features. So, before we add our next input type, it's time to refactor!

Refactoring is the practice of reorganizing code for maintenance, readability, and ease of use, while leaving its behavior unchanged. It's most often associated with the agile discipline of TDD (where the phrase "Red, Green, Refactor" was born), but it's a useful practice regardless of your specific development workflow. That said, refactoring is worlds easier when your production code is covered by a good suite of unit tests. And though I'm going to perform my refactor without a safety net now, I'll be covering unit testing, as well as some performance-driven refactoring in Chapters 4 and 5.

Refactoring Type Support

When refactoring JavaScript code, I prefer to think not just of the refactor that will benefit my current code, but the code I plan to add next. This might sound like a bit of "you ain't gonna need it" (or YAGNI) to you, but there are cases when I do indeed know "but I'm gonnna need it, and soon." (I tried to coin the acronym *BIGNIAS* for this, but it doesn't quite roll off the tongue.) Such is the case with my polyfill, where I know that much of the process of adding support for additional types will be consistent from one type to the next, with only a few, specific differences.

Because of this, the first step in my refactor is to move my `color` and `number` type upgrades into a *lookup table*, essentially just an array of objects that contains the type name and the upgrade function to execute for that type. My initial lookup object can be found in Example 3-12.

Example 3-12. Type lookup table for the `color` and `number` input types

```
var typeUpgrades = [
{
  type: 'color',
  upgrade: function(inputs) {
      inputs.kendoColorPicker({ palette: 'basic' });
  }
},
{
  type: 'number',
  upgrade: function(inputs) {
      inputs.kendoNumericTextBox();
  }
}];
```

Once I have my lookup table, I can refactor the code in Example 3-11 into something more like Example 3-13, where I iterate over each type in my lookup table, test for support, and perform the upgrade specified in the `upgrade` function for each.

Example 3-13. Using the lookup table to add input type support

```
var i, len;
for (i = 0, len = typeUpgrades.length; i < len; i++) {
  var typeObj = typeUpgrades[i];

  if (!isFormTypeSupported(typeObj.type)) {
    var inputs - form.find('input[type=' + typeObj.type + ']');
    typeObj.upgrade(inputs);
  }
}
```

If I rerun the sample page in a browser, I'll note that things still work just as before. That's nice, but the real benefit to refactoring comes when I add features to my polyfill, which I'll do next.

Before I move on, it's worth mentioning that refactoring doesn't have to stop with the simple changes I've detailed. While it's out of the scope of this short book to belabor the refactoring conversation any further, it's worth mentioning that, in the production version of my polyfill, I did perform some additional refactoring, including breaking my type upgrades and feature tests into two additional files, which I combine during my build process. If you're interested in seeing those additional changes, you can view the types (*http://bit.ly/typesjs*) and features (*http://bit.ly/featuresjs*) source files in the online GitHub repo (*http://bit.ly/kendo-ui*) for my polyfill.

Adding Input Types 3-*n*

Now that we've refactored things a bit, let's add support for a third input type: the range type. The range input type (*http://bit.ly/typerange*) enables developers to capture numeric data via a slider control with built-in min, max, and step values. Here's the text from section 4.10.7.1.14 in the HTML5 spec (*http://bit.ly/rangestate*):

Number State Section of the HTML5 Forms Spec
4.10.7.1.14 Range state

When an input element's type attribute is in the **Range** state, the rules in this section apply.

The input element represents a control for setting the element's value to a string representing a number, but with the caveat that the exact value is not important, letting UAs provide a simpler interface than they do for the Number state.

Note: In this state, the range and step constraints are enforced even during user input, and there is no way to set the value to the empty string.

If the element is mutable, the user agent should allow the user to change the number represented by its value, as obtained from applying the rules for parsing floating-point number values to it. User agents must not allow the user to set the value to a string that is not a valid floating-point number. If the user agent provides a user interface for selecting a number, then the value must be set to a best representation of the number representing the user's selection as a floating-point number. User agents must not allow the user to set the value to the empty string.

The value attribute, if specified, must have a value that is a valid floating-point number.

The value sanitization algorithm is as follows: If the value of the element is not a valid floating-point number, then set it to a valid floating-point number that represents the default value.

The min attribute, if specified, must have a value that is a valid floating-point number. The default minimum is 0. The max attribute, if specified, must have a value that is a valid floating-point number. The default maximum is 100.

The **default value** is the minimum plus half the difference between the minimum and the maximum, unless the maximum is less than the minimum, in which case the default value is the minimum.

When the element is suffering from an **underflow**, the user agent must set the element's value to a valid floating-point number that represents the minimum.

When the element is suffering from an **overflow**, if the maximum is not less than the minimum, the user agent must set the element's value to a valid floating-point number that represents the maximum.

The step scale factor is 1. The default step is 1 (allowing only integers, unless the min attribute has a noninteger value).

When the element is suffering from a step mismatch, the user agent must round the element's value to the nearest number for which the element would not suffer from a step mismatch, and which is greater than or equal to the minimum, and, if the maximum is not less than the minimum, which is less than or equal to the maximum. If two numbers match these constraints, then user agents must use the one nearest to positive infinity.

For example, the markup `<input type="range" min=0 max=100 step=20 value=50>` results in a range control whose initial value is 60.

The algorithm to convert a string to a number, given a string input, is as follows: If applying the rules for parsing floating-point number values to input results in an error, then return an error; otherwise, return the resulting number.

The algorithm to convert a number to a string, given a number input, is as follows: Return a valid floating-point number that represents input.

Bookkeeping details

The following common input element content attributes, IDL attributes, and methods apply to the element: `autocomplete`, `list`, `max`, `min`, and `step` content attributes; `list`, `value`, `valueAsNumber`, and `selectedOption` IDL attributes; `stepDown()` and `stepUp()` methods.

- The value IDL attribute is in mode value.
- The input and change events apply.
- The following content attributes must not be specified and do not apply to the element: accept, alt, checked, dirname, formaction, formenctype, formmethod, formno validate, formtarget, height, maxlength, multiple, pattern, placeholder, readonly, required, size, src, and width.
- The following IDL attributes and methods do not apply to the element: checked, files, selectionStart, selectionEnd, selectionDirection, and valueAsDate IDL attributes; select() and setSelectionRange() methods.

This is much more complex than the section for our color and number types, but there's some overlap with the number type, especially around attributes. Let's break this down into some rules, as we've done for the other two:

- The value attribute of an input with a type of range is a floating-point number.

- A valid range value is required at all times. If a valid range is not selected, the default value is used.

- The range value cannot be set to an empty string.

- If the user attempts to enter an invalid or non-numeric value, the input value should be set to the default value.

- The min attribute is allowed, and should represent a valid floating-point number. The default min value is 0.

- The max attribute is allowed, and should represent a valid floating-point number. The default max value is 100.

- The *default value* of the range input, if no value is set, is the minimum plus half the difference between the minimum and maximum: d = min + 0.5(max - min). If the default min and max values are used, the default value is 50: 0 + 0.5(100-0).

- When the set value is smaller than the minimum, the value should be automatically set to the minimum.

- When the set value is larger than the maximum, the value should be automatically set to the maximum.

- The step attribute is allowed and has a default value of 1, which allows only integers to be specified.

- If the value of the input is set programmatically and that value violates the specified step property (i.e., step is 20 and a value of 50 is set), the control should round the set value up to the closest value that matches the step and that does not violate the max attribute (in this example, the value would be set to 60).

In Kendo UI, the equivalent widget to the range type is the Slider (*http://bit.ly/slider cont*) control, which has identical behavior, and supports all of the necessary attributes and rules specified here. To add support for the range type, I'll add another object literal to my typeUpgrades array, as shown in Example 3-14.

Example 3-14. Adding support for the range input type

```
{
  type: 'range',
  upgrade: function(inputs) {
    inputs.kendoSlider({
      showButtons: false,
      tickPlacement: 'none'
    });
  }
}
```

For the Slider widget, I'll need to pass in a couple of configuration settings so that the default behavior of the Kendo UI Slider matches that of browsers that do support this type. That means no buttons or ticks. Just a simple slider, as depicted in Figure 3-5. And the best news is that there is no step 2, other than refreshing your browser and viewing the slider in the sample form! With the refactor that we made in the preceding section, adding support for additional input types is a simple matter of adding a new entry to our lookup table. Now, adding features 3–n is quick and painless.

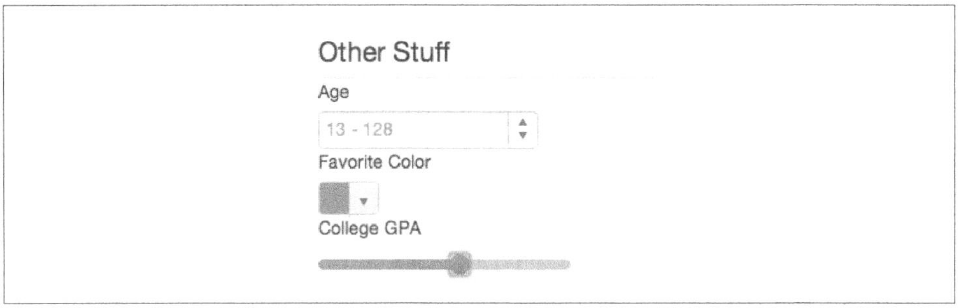

Figure 3-5. Sample form with range support

Building Utility Polyfills

When building your polyfill, you might, from time to time, encounter a situation where your polyfill needs a polyfill of its own. For instance, there are a bevy of JavaScript utility functions that, while useful, may not be supported in older browsers like IE6-8, which your polyfill will often need to target. Examples are useful utilities like `String.trim` and `Array.forEach`.

When developing your polyfill, you may encounter situations where some utility you need in the browser (such as a common JavaScript method) isn't supported. To address this, you can choose to either leverage some other approach that is supported across browsers, or you can build a polyfill for this utility.

If you choose to take the latter approach, I recommend taking a look at the Mozilla Developer Network (*https://developer.mozilla.org/*) which, in addition to having the best docs on the Web for frontend developers, is also a great resource for quick utility polyfills. For many of their JavaScript docs, MDN provides great information about current browser support, in addition to a quick snippet that can be used to polyfill support for that API across all browsers. An example can be seen in Example 3-15.

Example 3-15. A simple `Array.forEach` polyfill

```
if (!Array.prototype.forEach) {
  Array.prototype.forEach = function (fn, scope) {
    'use strict';
```

```
    var i, len;

    for (i = 0, len = this.length; i < len; ++i) {
      if (i in this) {
        fn.call(scope, this[i], i, this);
      }
    }
  };
}
```

This example is a simple polyfill for the `Array.forEach` method. First, I'll check for the existence of the `forEach` method on the `Array` prototype. If the method exists, we do nothing. If not, we'll add our polyfill, which is a simple `for` loop that iterates over each element of the array. For my HTML5 Forms polyfill, I've included this and other utility polyfills in a standalone source file that is included in my combined and minified production build.

Polyfilling Visual Features With CSS

With the input type refactor done, adding support for most of the remaining types (including `datetime`, `date`, `time`, and `month`) is pretty straightforward and not really worth covering in this book. There are a few quirks here and there with some of the date/time types, especially when it comes to the proper way to format date attribute values, but as long as you ensure you're properly handling date and time strings as covered in the spec (*http://bit.ly/datestring*), you should be fine. Your author failed to do so when he first started building his HTML5 Forms polyfill, so do take my word for it. Not coincidentally, it was this experience that lead yours truly to make "Read the Spec" the first principle of responsible polyfill development, as covered in Chapter 2.

Rather than covering the rest of the HTML5 input types explicitly, let's turn our focus to a different part of the HTML5 Forms spec, and take a look at a scenario where adding polyfill support requires JavaScript and CSS to get the job done. While there are a few areas of the HTML5 spec that require us to delve into CSS, the `placeholder` attribute is probably the best example of this type of feature. According to the Placeholder section of the spec (*http://bit.ly/placeholder-spec*), this attribute "represents a short hint (a word or short phrase) intended to aid the user with data entry when the control has no value." In contrast to the `<label>` element, the `placeholder` attribute is intended to contain hint text that is overlaid on or displayed inside input controls, and that disappears when a user enters a value.

Since the spec is pretty straightforward about this attribute, it enjoys pretty broad browser support. However, IE8 and previous don't support this attribute, and most of us still support these browsers in our sites and apps, so it makes sense to polyfill this feature in our library.

To do so, I'm going to start by adding a new CSS file in my project, under the *src/css/* directory, and I'll call it *kendo.forms.css*. Then, I'll add the CSS in Example 3-16.

Example 3-16. CSS for polyfilling placeholder support

```
label.placeholder {
    color: gray;
    display: block;
    font-size: small;
    padding-top: 3px;
    position: relative;
    text-indent: 5px;
}

input.placeholder {
    background-color: transparent;
    left: 0;
    position: absolute;
    top: 0;
    z-index: 1;
}

input.relPlaceholder {
    position: relative;
}

input.placeholder:focus, input.placeholder:first-line {
    background-color: white;
}

span.hidden {
    opacity: 0;
}
```

My strategy for polyfilling the `placeholder` will be to create a `<label>` that contains the same text as the `placeholder` attribute. The label will be overlaid on top of the input when the element is empty and does not have focus, and will be hidden when it does. The CSS is adding a few classes and pseudo elements that I'll need in order to manipulate elements that my polyfill will be creating at runtime. The `label.placeholder` selector applies to an element that I'll create to hold placeholder text, while the `input.place holder` selector applies to the original input for which I'm polyfilling attribute support. The remaining selectors cover positioning and visibility for elements and content.

With our CSS in place, I'll add the JavaScript needed for placeholder support. First, I'll need to add a feature test for this attribute in order to make sure that I don't do any unnecessary work (which will include some DOM interaction) if the browser already supports it. Since I know that this won't be the only attribute my polyfill will need to test for—it will also need to support new attributes like `required`, `pattern`, and more —I'll go ahead and create a generic test function, just as I did for the input types:

```
function isAttributeSupported(attr) {
  return attr in document.createElement('input') &&
         attr in document.createElement('textarea');
}
```

In the case of HTML5 attributes, testing for support is a simple matter of creating a new in-memory `input` (and `textarea`), and checking for the presence of an attribute via JavaScript's `in` property operator. If the attribute is available on both input types, our test will return `true`; otherwise, it returns `false`. Now we can leverage our test and, if not supported, add in some logic to activate placeholder support (as shown in Example 3-17).

Example 3-17. Polyfilling placeholder support with CSS and JavaScript

```
if(!isAttributeSupported('placeholder')) {
  form.find('[placeholder]').each(function(index, val) {
    var el = $(val);
    // Strip CR and LF from attribute vales, as specified in
    // www.w3.org/TR/html5/forms.html#the-placeholder-attribute
    var placeholderText = el.attr('placeholder').replace(/(\\r\\n|\\n|\\r)/gm,'');

    // When the field loses focus, clear out the placeholder if
    // the input contains a value.
    el.on('blur', function() {
      var $el = $(this);
      var labelNode = this.previousSibling;
      if (this.value) {
        labelNode.nodeValue = '';
        $el.addClass('relPlaceholder');
      } else if (labelNode.nodeValue !== placeholderText) {
        labelNode.nodeValue = placeholderText;
        $el.removeClass('relPlaceholder');
      }
    });
    el.wrap('<label class="placeholder">' + placeholderText + '</label>');
    el.addClass('placeholder');
  });
}
```

Let's walk through this sample step-by-step and take a look at what's going on. First, I'm grabbing all of the inputs with a `placeholder` attribute from my form. The rest of this block contains the callback for each placeholder-containing element. I start by caching the jQuery object for the element, and then grab the placeholder value. The RegEx on that line serves to strip out any newlines that might sneak into the placeholder attribute. This requirement is explicitly covered in the spec (*http://bit.ly/placeholder-spec*) and since we're polyfilling to the spec, it's a no-brainer to add this support.

Once I have a sanitized attribute value, I'll bind my element to a `blur` event, wrap my element in a new `<label>` that contains the placeholder text, and then add the `place holder` class to that label and the original element, which applies the CSS I defined in

Example 3-16. The CSS rules give my label some contrast so that it's obvious to the user that this is not input text (again, as per the spec) while also adding a rule to slide the label over to sit on top of my input.

The final piece of the puzzle is my blur event, which clears out the dummy placeholder label if the user has entered text in the input. Without this event, my placeholder text would show up over any text the user enters after navigating off the element.

Of course, this is all fine in theory, but as with every other feature we've had so far, it doesn't mean a thing until we test this new feature in a nonsupporting browser. However, since placeholder support is so darn good, it's not as simple as testing in one of the new browsers installed on your machine. Often, testing polyfill support means getting your hands on IE6, 7, or 8, and we'll discuss how to do that in the next section.

At this point, you might be wondering why we're switching gears to testing when we've not yet built our entire polyfill. We could go through the exercise of building the entire HTML5 Forms polyfill, but it's a mostly repetitive task now that we've covered the basics of input type support. There are other complexities to be solved, like forms validation, but in the interest of time and space in this short book, I decided to spend some time focusing on unit testing, performance, and refactoring over the next few chapters. These aspects of polyfill development are just as important as how you go about building the features themselves. That said, if you want to dig deeper into the guts of the HTML5 Forms polyfill we've started in this chapter, you're welcome to do so in the online repository (*http://bit.ly/kendo-ui*).

Testing Your Work Across Browsers

Thus far, we've been testing out our polyfill by viewing the sample HTML form in modern browsers like Chrome, Firefox, Opera, Safari, and IE9+. If you're following along, you've probably even been testing using just a single browser, which tends to be my own manual testing workflow as well. And while this strategy is fine when you're getting up and running and just trying to get things to work, eventually you're going to need to test in more than one browser. In fact, you're going to need to test in all of them, and often. In Chapter 4, I'll discuss some strategies for automating your cross-browser testing, but let's first look at a few ways that you can get started.

Installing the Evergreen Browsers

First, I recommend that you install every single browser that you can get your hands on for your OS. This might seem obvious, but it can't be overstated. When building cross-browser polyfills, you're venturing into the weeds so that other developers don't have to, so you'd better have access to every browser you can.

And I don't just mean the consumer release of every browser, but also the betas, dev channel, nightly releases, and platform previews of all of these. You need to know what your polyfill needs to support not only today, but tomorrow as well. Sometimes browser updates will modify their support for a feature in ways that will actually break your polyfill (spec API changes and vendor prefixes are two examples), and you'll want to be covered.

Modern, self-updating browsers are commonly referred to as *evergreen*, because they're always considered new and up-to-date. Nearly every major browser vendor now supports a self-updating model, and Table 3-2 lists all of these browsers and where to find them, as well as prerelease versions of these.

Table 3-2. Evergreen and prerelease desktop browsers

Browser	Update Cadence	Download URL
Chrome	~6 Weeks	*https://www.google.com/intl/en/chrome/browser/*
Chrome Beta	~6 Weeks	*https://www.google.com/intl/en/chrome/browser/beta.html*
Chrome Canary	Nightly	*https://www.google.com/intl/en/chrome/browser/canary.html*
Firefox	~6 Weeks	*https://www.mozilla.org/en-US/firefox/new/?icn=tabz*
Firefox Beta	~6 Weeks	*http://www.mozilla.org/en-US/firefox/beta/*
Firefox Nightly	Nightly	*http://nightly.mozilla.org/*
Internet Explorer	Varies	*http://windows.microsoft.com/en-us/internet-explorer/download-ie*
IE Platform Preview	Varies	*http://ie.microsoft.com/testdrive/*
Opera	Varies	*http://www.opera.com/*
Opera Next	Varies	*http://www.opera.com/computer/next*
Safari	Varies	*http://www.apple.com/safari/*
Safari Beta	Varies	*https://developer.apple.com/technologies/safari/*

While many of the names in this table are pretty straightforward, *Chrome Canary* isn't very self-explanatory. Canary is Google's "nightly" browser, which is updated once per day and represents the most cutting-edge work being done to Google Chrome.

Testing in OldIE

In addition to testing out your polyfill in the latest version of all of the browsers listed —not to mention mobile browsers if you're supporting those—I highly recommend hands-on testing with Internet Explorer 6, 7, and 8. If you're a Windows user, you might be tempted to use the Browser Mode and Document Mode features in IE's F12 Developer Tools to simulate IE7 and 8. I humbly ask that you resist that temptation but for the simplest of tests. These modes do a decent job of *simulating* the behaviors of oldIE, sure, but they aren't foolproof. For example, Figure 3-6 and Figure 3-7 illustrate the differences I see when running my HTML5 Forms polyfill test suite (which I'll introduce in the next chapter) in IE11, with simulation, and in IE8. It's the same code and same test suite for both, and even though Document Mode is providing me an IE8 experience in theory, you'll find that this is not always the case in practice.

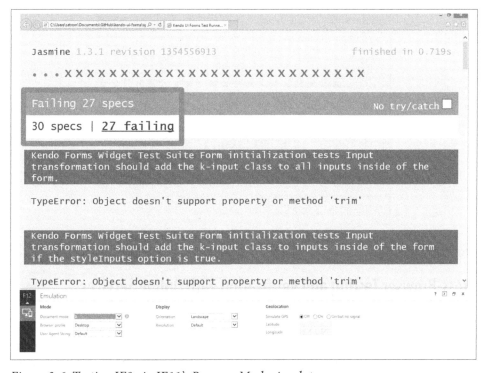

Figure 3-6. Testing IE8 via IE11's Browser Mode simulator

Thankfully, testing oldIE doesn't require that you buy old Windows Vista and XP licenses and install these browsers on the old hardware sitting in your closet. On the contrary, Microsoft hosts a fantastic site called modern.ie that's purpose-built around the idea of providing developers with all the tools they need to support and test the various Internet Explorer browsers. In addition to providing tools like a page-scanning service and documentation on standards support for newer versions of the browser, the site provides free virtual machines for testing all versions of IE, including 6, 7, and 8. Whether you use VirtualBox, VMWare, Parallels, Virtual PC, or Hyper-V, there are free VMs available for you to download, fire up, and use to test out your hard work. To grab a VM, just head over to modern.ie and click the "Test Across Browsers" menu option.

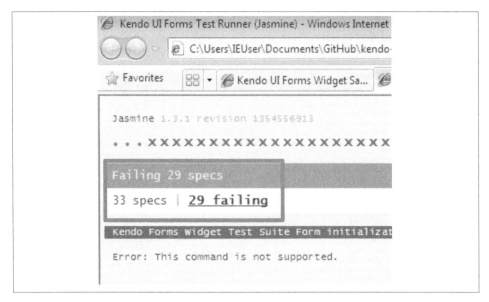

Figure 3-7. Testing IE8 via an actual IE8 installation

Cross-Browser Testing and Verification with Online Services

In addition to testing with your own browsers, and testing oldIE with VMs, there are a growing number of online services available that you can use to easily test your work across browsers without installing another browser or running a VM. One popular service is BrowserStack (*http://www.browserstack.com/*), which allows you to test public and internal URLs across a variety of OSs and browsers from within a browser window. You can also automate BrowserStack tests via Selenium for automated testing. The only catch with BrowserStack is that the service is not free, so it's not likely to be an option for most open source cross-browser polyfills.

Another great option for cross-browser testing is Testling (*http://ci.testling.com/*), a CI server that tests your code across browsers each time you push to your remote repo. Testling requires some form of automated unit test suite, but I consider this to be a plus because automated testing across the 18 versions Testling supports is far more ideal than manual tests, in my opinion. We'll discuss setting up unit and cross-browser tests in the next chapter.

In this chapter, we covered the basics of getting your polyfill project set up, and we also added basic features, did a simple refactor to improve polyfill maintenance, and even added support for the `placeholder` forms attribute in oldIE. We've come a long way already, and I hope you've learned a thing or two about putting those principles of responsible polyfill development into practice.

As great as our progress has been so far, though, you might find yourself bothered by the fact that a) our polyfill isn't terribly easy to test and b) we don't really have a strategy in place for linting our code, performing minification, or doing anything else that a good project should do before releasing production-quality code. In Chapter 4, we're going to cover all of these and more.

Building Your First Polyfill, Part 2: Build Workflows and Cross-Browser Testing

In Chapter 3, you got your first taste of cross-browser polyfill development via the construction of an HTML5 Forms polyfill. We managed to cover a lot of ground in a short time, but there's no doubt that our polyfill is missing some critical pieces. Some of these relate to our build and deploy process, while others relate to improving the quality and performance of the code itself with some unit and performance tests. Over these next two chapters, we'll round out the construction of our first polyfill. In this chapter, we'll cover the ins and outs of setting up your build process and performing automated testing. Then, in Chapter 5, we'll discuss how to deal with hairy edge cases in a spec, and testing/refactoring for performance.

Setting Up Your Project Workflow

In Chapter 3, we got right to work building our polyfill without considering much beyond simple project and source control setup. At this point, I'd like to back up and discuss some important workflow considerations that polyfill developers should address when starting up a project. Specifically, we want to begin with the end in mind. That is, before we write a single line of code, we should think about how we plan to distribute our hard work, and how we expect other developers to leverage our polyfill in their apps, and even how we can enable others to contribute to our project. All of these considerations can be addressed at the start of a project with a solid development workflow, which includes several core pieces:

- Source control and collaboration
- Package and dependency management
- Build and workflow management

- Automated and cross-browser testing
- Continuous integration

Source control and collaboration were discussed in Chapter 3, so let's look next at package and dependency management.

Package and Dependency Management

Once you've chosen a source control solution, you'll want to think about how to manage dependencies. By dependencies, I'm not referring to "this polyfill depends on jQuery," but, rather, the third-party libraries that your polyfill depends on for things like static analysis, minification, testing, and more. We'll talk about those specific tools in a bit, but before you start using these, you need to think about how you plan to include them in your project, and how to declare those dependencies for others who download your work. In the world of JavaScript development, there's no better general-purpose package manager than npm (*http://npmjs.org*), or node packaged modules. If you have Node.js installed, you already have npm. If not, head over to the Node.js site (*http://nodejs.org*) and grab the appropriate installer for your OS. You'll be using Node and npm heavily throughout your polyfill project, and these tools are also a prerequisite for the next few items on our list.

Build and Workflow Management

Developing open source software, including polyfills, is about more than just throwing together a quick sample, some basic tests, and a source file. Sure, it's possible to put something online that consists of only these things; I've even done it myself before. Five years ago, it was a common practice among frontend developers. But as our community has matured, our tools and our processes have evolved.

As a frontend developer, I have a workflow that's shared by many others. I write tests. I write code until those tests pass. I repeat. I test across browsers. I write some more code. During development, I keep my source files small and separate, but I want the code I distribute to be in a single file, minified and ready to use in production environments.

Executing all of these tasks—from testing to minification—by hand is a pain. Thankfully, there are great build and workflow tools out there for frontend devs. These tools, which you integrate into your project, can quickly perform these tasks on your behalf, either at your command or when a change to a project file is observed.

One such tool is Grunt (*http://gruntjs.com/*), a simple JavaScript task runner created by Ben Alman. Grunt is a bit of a youngster in the build system world, but it's caught fire among frontend developers and, with lots of community participation, has managed to achieve a good deal of stability in a short time.

I use Grunt in my projects and will do so in this book as well. The tool can be installed via npm (`npm install -g grunt-cli`). For more information, see the online getting started guide (*http://gruntjs.com/getting-started*). We'll walk through configuring an initial Grunt setup in a moment.

Automated and Cross-Browser Testing

If you're building a frontend library, testing is important, and it's vitally important if you're building a shim or polyfill. Almost every programming language out there has one or more options for unit testing, and JavaScript is no different. Unit testing (that is, the act of writing and executing code that exercises program code and performs assertions to verify that the program functioned as expected) has become quite popular over the last decade, especially in agile, eXtreme Programming, and Lean Software circles. Not only does unit testing aid developers in properly shaping the API and behavior of their libraries by writing code (via tests) in the mindset of the consumer, but a suite of tests, over time, serve as a wonderful safety net. With this net in place, developers are free to refactor, rework, and otherwise enhance their libraries, and remain confident in the fact that their tests will catch any regressions that fall through the cracks.

In the world of JavaScript development, there are countless unit-testing libraries. I prefer Jasmine (*http://bit.ly/jas-lib*), a BDD-style unit testing library. Other popular options include QUnit (*http://qunitjs.com*), which is maintained by the jQuery team, and NodeUnit (*http://bit.ly/nodeunit*).

Unit testing is a great foundation, but we also need to consider cross-browser testing for this project. It is a cross-browser polyfill, after all. As such, our project will also need to include an automated tool that can launch multiple browsers and load our unit tests up in each, thereby ensuring at least basic test coverage across browsers. The tool that I prefer to use for such a task is Karma (*http://bit.ly/karma-js*), which you can also install via npm. There's a bit of setup involved in getting Karma up and running the way I like, and we'll cover that in this chapter.

Continuous Integration

The last tool you should consider for your initial project setup is a remote CI server. This step is completely optional, so if you want to take my advice on items 1–4 and ignore me on this one, that's OK. That said, the biggest advantage of a remote CI server for an open source project is, in my mind, the ability to run basic project setup and unit tests in a clean environment. Doing so ensures that you properly declare dependencies via npm and that you never check in code that fails one or more tests and just walk away. It's better to get the news that you did something wrong from a CI server than from a human struggling to run the latest bits from your project.

For my projects, I prefer to use Travis (*https://travis-ci.org/*), a CI server used by many in the open source community. It's easy to set up and configure, and you can even place status badges on your project's home page signifying its current pass/fail status on the server. Another, newer option that I've recently discovered is Wercker (*http://werck er.com/*). I'll be using Travis for this book, but Wercker is certainly worth checking out for your next project, open source or otherwise.

Jump-Starting Your Workflow

In Chapter 3, I covered initial project setup, including a recommended directory structure and essential files. With your basic project structure in place, your next key workflow steps are to configure npm and Grunt, which we'll cover in this section.

Configuring npm

To configure npm, I'll run **npm init** inside my project directory and follow the interactive prompts. You can see the result of running the command in my terminal in Figure 4-1. Once done, npm will create a *package.json* file that looks similar to Example 4-1. While this file isn't strictly required unless you plan to publish your polyfill to npm, it will make it easier to work with Grunt, which we'll set up next.

Example 4-1. Sample package.json file

```
{
  "name": "html5-forms-polyfill",
  "version": "0.0.1",
  "description": "A cross-browser polyfill for HTML5 forms features",
  "repository": {
    "type": "git",
    "url": "git://github.com/bsatrom/html5-forms-polyfill.git"
  },
  "keywords": [
    "html5",
    "polyfill",
    "forms",
    "validation"
  ],
  "author": "Brandon Satrom",
  "license": "MIT",
  "readmeFilename": "README.md",
  "gitHead": "4a2f3578443f539d52c645563fe47824bf4fb377"
}
```

```
000                          1. satrom@web-dojo: ~/Dropbox/Development/html5-forms-polyfill (zsh)
  _ybilling-book (zsh)      _orms-polyfill (zsh)      _endo-ui-forms (zsh)
satrom@web-dojo ~/Dropbox/Development/html5-forms-polyfill$ npm init       master
This utility will walk you through creating a package.json file.
It only covers the most common items, and tries to guess sane defaults.

See `npm help json` for definitive documentation on these fields
and exactly what they do.

Use `npm install <pkg> --save` afterwards to install a package and
save it as a dependency in the package.json file.

Press ^C at any time to quit.
name: (html5-forms-polyfill)
version: (0.0.0) 0.0.1
description: A cross-browser polyfill for HTML5 forms features
entry point: (index.js)
test command: grunt test
git repository: (git://github.com/bsatrom/html5-forms-polyfill.git)
keywords: html5, polyfill, forms, validation
author: Brandon Satrom
license: (BSD) MIT
About to write to /Users/satrom/Dropbox/Development/html5-forms-polyfill/package.json
:

{
  "name": "html5-forms-polyfill",
  "version": "0.0.1",
  "description": "A cross-browser polyfill for HTML5 forms features",
  "main": "index.js",
  "scripts": {
    "test": "grunt test"
  },
  "repository": {
    "type": "git",
    "url": "git://github.com/bsatrom/html5-forms-polyfill.git"
  },
  "keywords": [
    "html5",
    "polyfill",
    "forms",
    "validation"
  ],
  "author": "Brandon Satrom",
  "license": "MIT",
  "readmeFilename": "README.md",
  "gitHead": "4a2f3578443f539d52c645563fe47824bf4fb377"
}
```

Figure 4-1. Running npm init to configure your package.json file

Configuring Grunt

Now, let's install Grunt. Before you run the Grunt config step, you'll need to add the following to your *package.json*, within the outer curly brace of the root object literal, and run npm install from the terminal. The settings in Example 4-2 will make sure that the Grunt command-line interface is available in your project.

Example 4-2. Grunt dependencies in package.json

```
"devDependencies": {
  "grunt": "~0.4.1",
  "grunt-contrib-jshint": "~0.6.0",
  "grunt-contrib-uglify": "~0.2.2",
  "grunt-contrib-concat": "~0.3.0",
  "grunt-contrib-cssmin": "~0.6.1"
}
```

Once you've installed Grunt, configuring the tool is a bit more manual. While there are several `grunt-init` tasks (*http://bit.ly/gruntscaff*) available, I find it easier to start with a very basic gruntfile, which you can pull from Example 4-3. Create a new file at the project root called *gruntfile.js* and copy the contents of Example 4-3 into that new file.

Example 4-3. Starter gruntfile.js for our polyfill

```
module.exports = function(grunt) {
  // Project configuration.
  grunt.initConfig({
    pkg: grunt.file.readJSON('package.json'),
    concat: {  ❶
      options: {
        separator: ';',
        banner: '// kendo-ui-forms v<%= pkg.version %> \n'
      },
      dist: {
        src: [ 'src/js/*.js' ],
        dest: 'dist/js/kendo.forms.js'
      }
    },
    uglify: {  ❷
      options: {
        banner: '// kendo-ui-forms v<%= pkg.version %> \n'
      },
      dist: {
        files: {
          'dist/js/kendo.forms.min.js': '<%= concat.dist.dest %>'
        }
      }
    },
    cssmin: {  ❸
      options: {
        banner: '// kendo-ui-forms v<%= pkg.version %> \n'
      },
      combine: {
        files: {
          'dist/css/kendo.forms.css': 'src/css/*.css'
        }
      },
      minify: {
        expand: true,
```

```
        cwd: 'src/css/',
        src: ['*.css', '!*.min.css'],
        dest: 'dist/css/',
        ext: '.forms.min.css'
      }
    },
    jshint: { ❹
      files: ['gruntfile.js', 'src/**/*.js', 'spec/js/*.js'],
      options: {
        globals: {
          jQuery: true,
          console: true,
          module: true,
          document: true
        }
      }
    }
  });

  // Plug-ins for other grunt tasks.
  grunt.loadNpmTasks('grunt-contrib-uglify');
  grunt.loadNpmTasks('grunt-contrib-jshint');
  grunt.loadNpmTasks('grunt-contrib-concat');
  grunt.loadNpmTasks('grunt-contrib-cssmin');

  // Default task(s).
  grunt.registerTask('default', ['jshint']);
  grunt.registerTask('minify', ['jshint', 'concat', 'cssmin', 'uglify']);
};
```

❶   Combines all of the JavaScript files in the *src/* directory into a single file

❷   Minifies the concatenated JavaScript file

❸   Combines and minifies any CSS files defined in *src/*

❹   Performs static analysis on my JavaScript source files to make sure I'm following a consistent coding style. See JSHint (*http://jshint.com*) for more information

Though it seems like there's a lot going on here, a gruntfile is pretty easy to parse once you get the hang of it. A gruntfile is made up of a series of named tasks, like concat, uglify, and the like. Each task tells Grunt what actions to perform, and which files to perform those actions on when that task is executed.

At the bottom of my gruntfile, I've also defined two additional tasks: a default task, which runs when I execute the grunt command with no other task, and a custom minify command, which is a combination of several commands defined in the preceding code.

Once your gruntfile is complete and the options match your project, run grunt from the terminal. If your gruntfile checks out, you'll get a "Done, without errors" message, which means we can continue on! If not, Grunt will point you in the direction of the problem, which is usually a minor syntax issue. Now, let's get some unit tests set up!

Adding Unit Tests to Your Polyfill

Testing is critical for a good, "responsible" polyfill, and I recommend that your own project be covered by a good set of unit tests. Testing frameworks like Jasmine and QUnit are easy to set up and configure and, once you get going with them, you'll be glad that you have a full suite of tests backing up your polyfill development.

Configuring Unit Tests with Jasmine

To start using Jasmine for my unit tests, I'll create a *lib* directory inside my *spec/* directory and place the Jasmine bits inside. I'm also going to include the jasmine-jquery (*http:// bit.ly/jas-jq*) library, which I'll need in order to automatically execute my tests.

Next, I'll create a *runner.html* file at the root of the *spec/* folder, and I'll populate it with the contents of Example 4-4. Many JavaScript frameworks, Jasmine included, use an HTML file as their test runner by loading up dependencies and the project source, and then executing those tests against DOM interactions on the page. On this page, we'll specify all of the CSS and JavaScript dependencies for our polyfill, including jQuery and Kendo UI for widgets and framework features, and then load up our tests via *fixtures.js*. Note that, for external dependencies, I'm following the directory structure outlined in Chapter 3.

Example 4-4. Jasmine's main runner.html file

```
<!DOCTYPE html>
<html>
  <head>
    <title>Kendo UI Forms Test Runner (Jasmine)</title>
    <meta charset="UTF-8">
    <!-- Styles -->
    <link rel="shortcut icon" type="image/png"
      href="lib/jasmine-1.3.1/jasmine_favicon.png">
    <link rel="stylesheet" type="text/css" href="lib/jasmine-1.3.1/jasmine.css">
    <link rel="stylesheet" href="../lib/css/kendo.common.min.css" />
    <link rel="stylesheet" href="../lib/css/kendo.default.min.css" /> ❶

    <!-- Jasmine and Jasmine-jQuery -->
    <script type="text/javascript" src="lib/jasmine-1.3.1/jasmine.js"></script>
    <script type="text/javascript" src="lib/jasmine-1.3.1/jasmine-html.js"></script>
    <script src="../lib/js/jquery.min.js"></script>
    <script type="text/javascript" src="lib/jasmine-jquery.js"></script>

    <!-- Kendo UI -->
    <script src="../lib/js/kendo.web.min.js"></script> ❷
    <script src="../src/js/kendo.forms.js"></script> ❸
```

```
  <!-- Specs -->
  <script src="js/fixtures.js"></script> ❹
</head>
<body>
  <!-- Jasmine -->
  <script type="text/javascript">
    (function() {
      var jasmineEnv = jasmine.getEnv();
      jasmineEnv.updateInterval = 1000;

      var htmlReporter = new jasmine.HtmlReporter();

      jasmineEnv.addReporter(htmlReporter);

      jasmineEnv.specFilter = function(spec) {
        return htmlReporter.specFilter(spec);
      };

      var currentWindowOnload = window.onload;

      window.onload = function() {
        if (currentWindowOnload) {
          currentWindowOnload();
        }
        execJasmine();
      };

      function execJasmine() {
        jasmineEnv.execute();
      }

    })();
  </script>
</body>
</html>
```

❶   These two lines include the Kendo UI CSS styles

❷   The main source file for Kendo UI Web, which our polyfill needs for UI widgets
      and framework features

❸   This is the main source file for our polyfill

❹   This file contains all of our test fixtures

With the runner done, let's create the key file for our testing, *fixtures.js*. Example 4-5
contains an initial test file with a couple of tests. You'll notice that Jasmine uses functions
like describe, it, and expect, and that my test names are written in narrative form.
Because Jasmine is a BDD-style testing framework, you'll hopefully find, as I do, that
it's easy to write readable test names and assertions that make sense, not just now, but
when you're hunting down regressions later.

Example 4-5. A basic Jasmine fixtures.js file for our polyfill

```
describe('Kendo Forms Widget Test Suite', function() {
  describe('Form initialization tests', function() {
    describe('Form Widget initialization', function() {
      it('should exist in the kendo.ui namespace', function() {
        expect(kendo.ui.Form).toBeDefined();
      });

      it('should be able to perform imperative initialization with JavaScript', function() {
        expect($('#imperative-form').kendoForm).toBeDefined();
      });

    });
  });
});
```

With this setup done, let's go ahead and run these tests in the browser. First, if you're following along and you created the *kendo.forms.js* source file in Chapter 3, the preceding tests should pass. That's nice, but for the sake of exploration, let's delete everything from that file and rerun our tests. If Jasmine is properly configured, you should see two failing tests, as we do in Figure 4-2. So we have successfully configured our testing framework. Now, let's go make these tests pass!

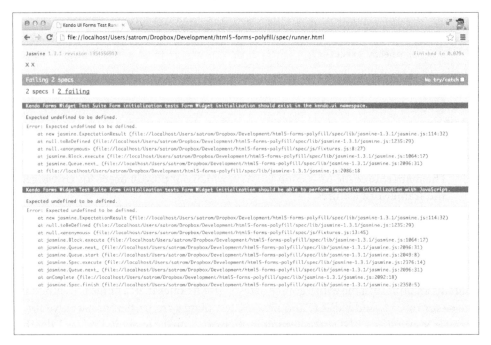

Figure 4-2. Jasmine running in the browser

Red to Green: Making the First Tests Pass

When I start a new project, or add unit tests to an existing project, I like to start small and try to get a few quick win tests under my belt. This is partly because I'm still feeling out functionality in the early stages of a project, but also because I want to see my test suite running and passing as quickly as possible. It's far easier to suss out problems with my test suite setup with a smaller number of tests.

With that in mind, the first two failing specs we've added to my project are minor and easy to fix, but they help lay the foundation for my polyfill. As discussed in Chapter 3, Kendo UI itself exposes its UI widgets to developers in two ways, and the preceding tests are designed to exercise that behavior. The tests in Example 4-5 are looking for key pieces of information. First, we check to make sure that our polyfill exists as a widget in the Kendo UI namespace, as `kendo.ui.Form`. Next, we want to ensure that the polyfill widget is available as a jQuery plug-in. To make those tests pass, we can create the initial skeleton of our polyfill in a new file (in *src/*) called *kendo.forms.js* and add the code in Example 4-6, or add the code back in if you already did so in Chapter 3.

Example 4-6. Creating the core widget definition for our Kendo UI Forms polyfill in kendo.forms.js

```
(function($, kendo) {
  var ui = kendo.ui,
    Widget = ui.Widget,
    formWidget;

  var Form = Widget.extend({
    init: function(element, options) {
      // base call to widget initialization
      Widget.fn.init.call(this, element, options);
    },
    options: {
      // the name is what will appear in the kendo namespace (kendo.ui.Form).
      // The jQuery plug-in would be jQuery.fn.kendoForm.
      name: 'Form'
    }
  });

  ui.plugin(Form);
} (jQuery, kendo));
```

We added a lot more code to this file in Chapter 3 before all was said and done, but this skeleton code we've written so far lays the foundation for my library, and it's also enough to make my first tests pass, as you can see in Figure 4-3.

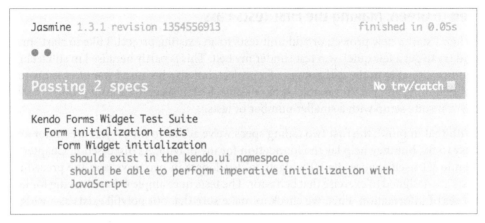

```
Jasmine 1.3.1 revision 1354556913                    finished in 0.05s

● ●

Passing 2 specs                                          No try/catch ▣

Kendo Forms Widget Test Suite
  Form initialization tests
    Form Widget initialization
      should exist in the kendo.ui namespace
      should be able to perform imperative initialization with
      JavaScript
```

Figure 4-3. Basic Jasmine tests passing

Running Jasmine Tests via Grunt

So far, we've gotten Jasmine configured for our unit tests, and we've even gotten a couple of failing tests to pass. This is a great start, but all of our work is in the browser, and running our tests requires that we refresh a browser tab to verify. This is probably fine for many projects, but I'd like to be able to execute my tests in both the browser and via the command line, the latter of which is required when I start working with Karma and Travis CI later. This also allows me to streamline my development workflow by auto-matically running tests whenever I save certain files in my project.

Thankfully, I'm not alone in my desire for console-based JavaScript testing, and there just so happens to be a Grunt plug-in for Jasmine that I can add to my project. First, I'll want to configure Jasmine by adding a few lines to my gruntfile. I'll add the `grunt-contrib-jasmine` task declaration to the bottom of the file, like so:

```
grunt.loadNpmTasks('grunt-contrib-jasmine');
```

Then, I need to add a Jasmine task to the `initConfig` section of the file, as shown in Example 4-7. This task definition tells Jasmine where to look to find my project source, the specs to run, and finally, any third-party vendor libraries that should also be loaded.

Example 4-7. Adding a Jasmine Grunt task to gruntfile.js

```
jasmine: {
  src: ['lib/**/*.js', 'src/js/kendo.forms.utils.js',
    'src/js/kendo.forms.types.js',
    'src/js/kendo.forms.features.js',
    'src/js/kendo.forms.js'
  ],
  options: {
    specs: 'spec/js/*.js',
    vendor: [
```

```
      'spec/lib/jasmine-jquery.js'
    ]
  }
}
```

Next, I'll want to install the Jasmine Grunt plug-in via the following terminal command:

```
npm install grunt-contrib-jasmine --save-dev
```

Once I've done so, I can run the command `grunt jasmine` via the console, and I'll get a result that looks like Example 4-8.

 The `--save-dev` switch will automatically save the package as a development dependency in your *package.json* file, ensuring that other devs and your CI environment can quickly replicate your setup.

Example 4-8. Running Jasmine via the console

```
$ grunt jasmine
Running "jasmine:src" (jasmine) task
Testing jasmine specs via phantom

..
2 specs in 0.001s.
>> 0 failures

Done, without errors.
```

Now I've got Jasmine running in the browser, and in the terminal, which is nice! Unfortunately, our configuration work isn't quite done yet. Everything works great so far because neither of our initial tests access the DOM. Once we need to access the DOM, though, things get a bit tricky, so I'll need to add a little more configuration to keep this happy testing party going.

Let's add our third test, and the first to access the DOM. I'll open *fixtures.js* back up and add the test in Example 4-9.

Example 4-9. Testing declarative form initialization in fixtures.js

```
it('should be able to perform declarative initialization with data attributes',
  function() {
  kendo.init(document.body);

  expect($('#declarative-form').data('kendoForm')).not.toBe(null);
});
```

As discussed previously, Kendo UI widgets can be declared one of two ways: either using JavaScript, or via `data-role` declaration and calling `kendo.init` on a container, which creates widgets for every element inside that container. The preceding test calls kendo.init on document.body, which will look for every element with a data-role attribute, and initialize that element accordingly.

When I first add this test and refresh the browser, it will fail, but I can make it pass by adding the code in Example 4-10 to the *runner.html* file, just inside the <body> element.

Example 4-10. Declarative initialization of a Form widget in runner.html

```
<form id="declarative-form" data-role="form"></form>
```

Configuring Jasmine for the Browser and the Console

After adding the markup in Example 4-10, all three of my tests will pass. That's nice, but in the spirit of keeping our test options open, let's rerun the grunt jasmine command and see what happens. Spoiler alert: it looks like Figure 4-4. That's a failing test. Why did our test fail in my terminal, even though it worked in the browser? The answer lies in the DOM, or lack thereof, that is. When I'm using Jasmine via the console, there is no DOM available for my tests, so in order to leverage the DOM for testing, I need to do a bit of additional setup. For that, I'll use the jasmine-jquery (*http://bit.ly/jas-jq*) library, which allows me to load HTML files into my specs and execute my tests against them.

```
satrom@web-dojo ~/Dropbox/Development/html5-forms-polyfill$ grunt jasmine    ★master
Running "jasmine:src" (jasmine) task
Testing jasmine specs via phantom
..X
Kendo Forms Widget Test Suite:: Form initialization tests:: Form Widget initializatio
n:: should be able to perform declarative initialization with data attributes: failed
  Expected null not to be null. (1)
3 specs in 0.002s.
>> 1 failures
Warning: Task "jasmine:src" failed. Use --force to continue.

Aborted due to warnings.
```

Figure 4-4. Running Jasmine DOM tests in the console

First, I'll need to move the form tag from Example 4-10 into a standalone HTML file named *declarative-form.html*, and I'll place that file in a *spec/javascripts/fixtures/* directory—the location is a convention jasmine-jquery uses. Then, I need to add the jasmine-jquery fixture loader to my *fixtures.js* file, so I'll add the path shown in Example 4-11 to line 4.

Example 4-11. Setup for loading external fixtures from fixtures.js

```
var fixtures = jasmine.getFixtures();
if (document.location.pathname.indexOf('runner.html') > 0) {
  // We're running jasmine in the browser
  fixtures.fixturesPath = '../spec/javascripts/fixtures';
}
```

In order to run Jasmine in multiple environments, I do have to add a bit of path manipulation, as you can see in the preceding sample. If I'm running my tests in the console, the default path (*spec/javascripts/fixtures*) works for loading fixtures. If I'm in the browser, however, I need to adjust things a little. Finally, in my latest test, Example 4-9, I'll add a call to jasmine-jquery's load method to load up my HTML fixture. The complete test is listed in Example 4-12.

Example 4-12. Loading an external fixture from fixtures.js

```
it('should be able to perform declarative initialization with data attributes',
  function() {
    fixtures.load('declarative-form.html');

    kendo.init(document.body);

    expect($('#declarative-form').data('kendoForm')).not.toBe(null);
});
```

When I rerun `grunt jasmine` in the console, I should see all green. I can also rerun the tests in my browser, where everything also passes with flying colors.

I now have a complete unit test setup that works in the browser and via the console, which is about to come in quite handy!

Automating Cross-Browser Polyfill Testing

Now that we have a good testing setup with Jasmine and Grunt, let's take this party to the next level and add in some cross-browser testing. While automated cross-browser testing might be considered overkill for some types of projects, it's a must when building a polyfill. As you build your polyfill, you'll quickly discover cases where a certain test isn't needed in your everyday development browser because the feature is present, but the feature still needs a good solid test because your polyfill provides capabilities for another browser to leverage. Performing automated testing across several installed browsers can be a quick sanity check to ensure that development of your polyfill is progressing along without a hitch and, thankfully, there are some great tools out there that we can pair with our existing Grunt workflow. My tool of choice is Karma (*http://bit.ly/karma-js*), a simple test runner that can call out to all major browsers using test runner plug-ins and also integrates nicely with Grunt.

 As I discussed in Chapter 3, automated cross-browser testing is a great safety net for the polyfill developer, but it's no substitute for real, actual testing across browsers, especially those older versions of IE, where browser quirks lie in wait.

Configuring Cross-Browser Tests with Karma

To get started with Karma, I'll need to install `grunt-karma` via npm:

```
npm install grunt-karma --save-dev
```

Both Karma and grunt-karma will be installed, and a series of Karma-related dependencies will be added to your *package.json* file. Next, you'll want to add the line `grunt.loadNpmTasks(`*grunt-karma*`);` to the end of the `loadNpmTasks` calls in your gruntfile. Then, I'll add the Karma task to my gruntfile, starting with a bit of logic to populate an array of browsers I want to test with, at the top of the file, as shown in Example 4-13.

Example 4-13. Adding a browser array to gruntfile.js

```
var browsers;
(function() {
  var os = require('os');
  browsers = ['Chrome', 'Firefox', 'Opera'];
  if (os.type() === 'Darwin') {
    browsers.push('ChromeCanary');
    browsers.push('Safari');
  }
  if (os.type() === 'Windows_NT') {
    browsers.push('IE');
  }
})();
```

In this snippet, I'm using Node to figure out which OS I'm testing. If I'm using OS X (which reports as *Darwin*), I'll add Chrome Canary and Safari. If, on the other hand, I'm on Windows, I'll add IE to my browsers array.

 Both Internet Explorer and, recently, Safari are single-OS browsers, meaning that they run only on Windows and Mac OS X, respectively. This means that it's not possible to run a complete set of cross-browser tests for your polyfills on a single OS. You'll need either a few Windows VMs on hand for various versions of IE, or a cheap Mac OS X box for Safari testing if either of these is not your primary operating system.

Next, I'll add a task for Karma to the `grunt.initConfig` method, as shown in Example 4-14:

Example 4-14. Adding a Karma task to gruntfile.js

```
karma: {
  options: {
    configFile: 'conf/karma.conf.js',
```

```
    keepalive: true
  },
  forms: {
    browsers: browsers
  }
}
```

Key in this section is the `configFile` property, which accepts a path to a separate Karma configuration file. Karma has a lot of configuration options, so placing these in a separate file is usually a good approach. The contents of my *karma.conf.js* can be found in Example 4-15.

Example 4-15. karma.conf.js Karma configuration file for our forms polyfill

```
module.exports = function(config) {
  config.set({
    // base path that will be used to resolve files and exclude
    basePath: '../',

    // list of files / patterns to load in the browser
    files: [
      'lib/js/*.js',
      'dist/js/kendo.forms.min.js',
      {pattern: 'lib/js/jquery.min.js', watched: false, served: true,
        included: true},
      {pattern: 'spec/lib/jasmine-jquery.js', watched: false, served: true,
        included: true},
      {pattern: 'src/js/*.js', watched: true, served: true,
        included: false},
      {pattern: 'spec/**/*.html', included: false},
      'spec/js/*.js',
    ],

    // list of files to exclude
    exclude: [],

    frameworks: ['jasmine'],
    reporters: ['progress'],
    port: 9876,
    runnerPort: 9100,
    colors: true,
    logLevel: config.LOG_INFO,
    autoWatch: true,

    browsers: ['ChromeCanary'],
    captureTimeout: 50000,
    singleRun: true,
    reportSlowerThan: 500,
    preprocessors: {},

    plugins: [
      'karma-jasmine',
```

```
      'karma-chrome-launcher',
      'karma-firefox-launcher',
      'karma-safari-launcher',
      'karma-opera-launcher',
      'karma-ie-launcher',
      'karma-script-launcher'
    ]
  });
};
```

This file contains a couple of key sections. First, the `files` array contains all of the source files from my project that Karma needs to know about in order to properly execute my tests. Next, I include a series of options regarding the test runner (Jasmine), which ports to use, and the like. Finally, I specify a series of Karma plug-ins, which the framework needs to communicate with my test runner and browsers. By default, Karma includes the launchers for Firefox and Chrome, so I'll need to install the Opera, Safari, and IE launchers to use them:

```
npm install karma-opera-launcher --save-dev
npm install karma-safari-launcher --save-dev
npm install karma-ie-launcher --save-dev
```

Making Karma, Jasmine, and the Browser Play Nice

Once I've installed those two additional launchers, I should be able to run Karma using Grunt with the `grunt karma` command. If I do that, I should see all of my browsers launch, but one of my three initial tests will fail. Can you guess which ones? That's right, the DOM test. Much as I did for Jasmine in the console, I need to add a path condition for Karma to my *fixtures.js* file, as shown in Example 4-16.

Example 4-16. Modifying the fixtures.js external fixtures load path for Karma

```
if (document.location.pathname === '/context.html') {
  // Karma is running the test, so change the base
  fixtures.fixturesPath = 'base/spec/javascripts/fixtures';
} else if (document.location.pathname.indexOf('runner.html') > 0) {
  // We're running jasmine in the browser
  fixtures.fixturesPath = '../spec/javascripts/fixtures';
}
```

With this additional condition, I'm looking for *context.html* in my path, which is the environment under which Karma runs. If that value is found, I'll adjust the base `fix turesPath` to account for the location from which Karma loads these files. Otherwise, I'll look for my in-browser *runner.html*, as before. And that's it. I can return to the console and run `grunt karma` and watch all my tests pass in five browsers, as shown in Figure 4-5. It's a thing of beauty!

```
satrom@web-dojo ~/Dropbox/Development/html5-forms-polyfill$ grunt karma
Running "karma:forms" (karma) task
WARN [karma]: Port 9876 in use
WARN [karma]: Port 9877 in use
WARN [karma]: Port 9878 in use
INFO [karma]: Karma v0.10.1 server started at http://localhost:9879/
INFO [launcher]: Starting browser Chrome
INFO [launcher]: Starting browser Firefox
INFO [launcher]: Starting browser Opera
INFO [launcher]: Starting browser ChromeCanary
INFO [launcher]: Starting browser Safari
INFO [Firefox 20.0.0 (Mac OS X 10.8)]: Connected on socket id OL6iBvRsTWH30sKhhn2_
INFO [Safari 6.0.5 (Mac OS X 10.8.4)]: Connected on socket id ctKjiK_TAyZZBFlMhn3A
INFO [Chrome 29.0.1547 (Mac OS X 10.8.4)]: Connected on socket id BefGH-xvTECSVWWEhn2
9
INFO [Chrome 31.0.1600 (Mac OS X 10.8.4)]: Connected on socket id YgKcGPVBqpbBJybIhn2
~
INFO [Opera 12.10.0 (Mac OS X 10.8.4)]: Connected on socket id 2SokUQi4PLtL5qeYhn3B
Firefox 20.0.0 (Mac OS X 10.8): Executed 3 of 3 SUCCESS (0.51 secs / 0.037 secs)
Safari 6.0.5 (Mac OS X 10.8.4): Executed 3 of 3 SUCCESS (0.41 secs / 0.06 secs)
Chrome 29.0.1547 (Mac OS X 10.8.4): Executed 3 of 3 SUCCESS (0.641 secs / 0.077 secs)
Chrome 31.0.1600 (Mac OS X 10.8.4): Executed 3 of 3 SUCCESS (0.624 secs / 0.067 secs)
Opera 12.10.0 (Mac OS X 10.8.4): Executed 3 of 3 SUCCESS (1.1 secs / 0.014 secs)
TOTAL: 15 SUCCESS

Done, without errors.
```

Figure 4-5. Running cross-browser tests with Karma

Automating Polyfill Development with Grunt Tasks

Thus far in this chapter, we've set up a new polyfill project, we've configured npm and Grunt for our development workflow, and we've added Jasmine and Karma for unit and cross-browser testing. All of these moving pieces work great alone, but we're now going to bring them together for a killer polyfill development workflow. As mentioned earlier, Grunt gives you the ability to create custom tasks that chain together predefined tasks in interesting ways. One example is the minify task in Example 4-3, which automatically runs JSHint, concatenates your source files, and then runs uglifyJS to minify them.

Now that we've added some testing, let's add a few more custom tasks that combine our test frameworks with our JSHint and magnification tasks, as shown in Example 4-17.

Example 4-17. Adding tasks to gruntfile.js

```
grunt.registerTask('test', ['minify', 'jasmine']);
grunt.registerTask('x-test', ['minify', 'jasmine', 'karma:forms']);
```

Now I can run grunt test in the console and have my files linted, minified, combined, and tested, or I can run grunt x-test, which will do all of the above and then run my tests across all browsers using Karma.

Linting is the practice of checking source code for syntax errors or style violations. In the JavaScript space, two popular code-linting tools are JSLint (*http://jslint.com*) and JSHint (*http://jshint.com*).

While task customization is nice, what I'd really like to be able to do is execute a Grunt command once, and have that command watch my source files for changes. Then, when one of those files is saved, Grunt will execute one or more tasks automatically. Sounds awesome, right? It is, and with Grunt, it's built in. All I need is the `grunt-contrib-watch` plug-in, which I can install via npm:

```
npm install grunt-contrib-watch --save-dev
```

Once I've installed this plug-in, I'll include the task via a call to `loadNpmTasks`:

```
grunt.loadNpmTasks('grunt-contrib-watch');
```

And finally, I'll add the task to `grunt.initConfig`:

```
watch: {
  scripts: {
    files: ['<%= jshint.files %>'],
    tasks: ['test'],
    options: {
      nospawn: true
    }
  }
}
```

Now I can run `grunt watch` before I begin working on my polyfill. As I make changes to important files, Grunt will pick those up, lint the files, and run my Jasmine tests automatically, as shown in Figure 4-6.

```
satrom@web-dojo ~/Dropbox/Development/html5-forms-polyfill$ grunt watch        master
Running "watch" task
Waiting...
Reloading watch config...

Running "watch" task
Waiting...OK
>> File "gruntfile.js" changed.
>> File "src/js/kendo.forms.js" changed.


Running "jshint:files" (jshint) task
>> 2 files lint free.

Running "concat:dist" (concat) task
File "dist/js/kendo.forms.js" created.

Running "uglify:dist" (uglify) task
File "dist/js/kendo.forms.min.js" created.

Running "jasmine:src" (jasmine) task
Testing jasmine specs via phantom
...
3 specs in 0.003s.
>> 0 failures

Running "watch" task
Completed in 2.014s at Wed Aug 14 2013 16:01:45 GMT-0500 (CDT) - Waiting...
```

Figure 4-6. Developing iteratively with `grunt watch`

Performing Remote Testing with Travis CI

Before we wrap up this chapter, there's one final piece of setup I suggest you perform when building a cross-browser polyfill: configuring a CI server to run your tests and provide you with that extra-level sanity check. As I said previously, I prefer Travis CI because the service is free for open source projects, and it's dead-simple to configure. In fact, all I need in my project is to add a file called *.travis.yml* with a few options, as shown in Example 4-18.

Example 4-18. A Travis CI configuration file, .travis.yml, for our Forms polyfill

```
language: node_js
node_js:
  - "0.10"
  - "0.8"
before_script:
  - npm install -g grunt-cli
```

This file, which I'll include in my Git repository and push to GitHub, tells Travis that I'm running a NodeJS app, and that I'd like to test it using Node v0.10 and v0.8. I've also included the `before_script` option to ensure that the CI server has the Grunt CLI installed, which I need to run my tests. Once I've added this file and pushed it to GitHub,

I can head over to the Travis website (*http://travis-ci.org*) and follow their Getting Started guide (*http://bit.ly/trav-started*) to configure my project with their service.

Once everything is set up, any time I push a commit to my repo from GitHub to Travis, the service will spin up and run my tests, giving me that extra measure of defense for my polyfill. Figure 4-7 shows an example status screen for my HTML5 Forms polyfill. Looks like a success!

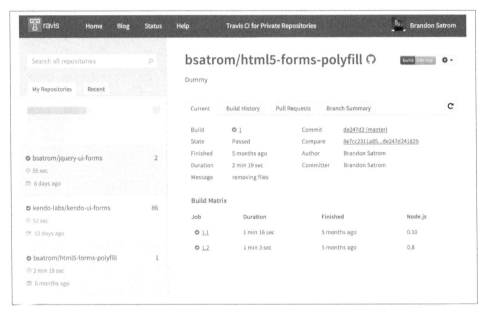

Figure 4-7. The Travis dashboard with test results for our polyfill

Since there are so many moving pieces involved in getting cross-browser testing set up, I've purposely kept our fixtures file small, covering only three tests. However, the full kendo-ui-forms polyfill contains a much larger test suite, and I suggest you check it out for yourself (*http://bit.ly/fixturejs*) when venturing into testing for your own polyfills.

The Bottom Line: Use What Works for You!

We've covered a ton of ground in this chapter, and while much of it is not specific to polyfill development, I felt this chapter was an important one to include because a great polyfill needs tests—and lots of 'em—and a rock-solid development workflow. As you'll see in the next chapter, polyfill development can get hairy at times, especially as you delve into oldIE, so the more thorough your tests and your workflow, the better off you'll be as you head down the narrow road.

In this chapter, I mentioned a lot of third-party and open source technologies that I prefer to use when building polyfills. Some of these might work for you as well, while in other cases you have a personal favorite you like to use. That's OK! All that matters is that you get a good dev and test workflow in place early on, no matter which tools you choose to use.

Now that our development and testing workflow is in place and we've built a nice cross-browser polyfill, let's take a look at edge cases, performance considerations, and finally, how to release your polyfill into the wild.

CHAPTER 5

Building Your First Polyfill, Part 3: Performance and Edge-Case Testing

Over the last two chapters, we've built a pretty nice cross-browser polyfill from the ground up, and we've even added a complete testing setup to ensure that your library always works as expected. So while Chapters 3 and 4 were about making sure that your polyfill works, this chapter is about making sure that it works well. In particular, we're going to discuss optimizing your polyfill for performance, as well as how to handle quirky, browser-specific edge cases that can reveal themselves from time to time.

Building for Performance

In Chapter 2, I introduced several principles of responsible polyfill development. One of these was "Build with performance in mind." The spirit of this principle is to encourage polyfill developers to go beyond only delivering a functional equivalent to a native browser feature via their library, but to ensure that this equivalent is also as fast as it can possibly be.

This is a high bar, for sure. Your polyfill's performance baseline is the native rendering capabilities of the browser. Chances are, your library won't be able to match the speed of a native feature, and attempting to do so should not be your focus. Instead, you should instead strive to pass the frontend developers' *noticeability* test. It's a simple test. If, after including your library in a developer's application, that app runs noticeably slower, you can expect that your polyfill will be dropped on the floor, quickly. That, or the developer will contact you and complain. Remember, polyfills are designed to emulate native browser capabilities, so you should consider it your solemn duty *not* to be noticed by developers, or end users, for that matter. And while the noticeability test itself is both far from scientific and something that varies from developer to developer, there are some strategies you can adopt to increase the chances that you'll pass this test:

1. Setup performance benchmarks.

2. Don't execute code too early or too often.

3. Iterate until you're happy and then iterate some more.

We'll look at each of these, in turn.

1. Set Up Performance Benchmarks

First things first: if you want to build for performance, you need to be able to test and assess the performance of your polyfill. You certainly *could* eyeball it and judge your library by how fast it "feels" to you, but I suggest being a bit more intentional if you can stand it. Specifically, I suggest using JSPerf (*http://jsperf.com*) to benchmark and test your polyfill, not only at the start, but as you continue to iterate and make changes. JSPerf, which is based on the open source Benchmark.js library (*http://bench markjs.com*), is a quick and easy way to set up tests of your library's features and functionality. Alternatively, you *could* use Benchmark.js directly, the grunt-benchmark Grunt plug-in (*http://bit.ly/grunt-ben*), or just use the DevTools in your favorite browser to run ad hoc tests, but I find that JSPerf has everything I need to run performance tests and comparisons across revisions to my polyfills. Plus, it has pretty charts, courtesy of Browserscope (*http://browserscope.org*). In the next section, I'll walk through setting up a simple JSPerf test to show the delta after a simple tweak to my polyfill.

2. Don't Execute Code Too Early or Too Often

The next strategy we can employ to pass the noticeability test is to make sure that our polyfill doesn't execute any code it doesn't have to. This is especially important if your library is a drop-in or opt-in polyfill that performs its own feature detection. For instance, our HTML5 Forms polyfill needs to test for browser support of several input types. In Chapter 3, we perform feature detection as we loop over each input in a form, as shown in Example 5-1.

Example 5-1. Form support with feature detection in kendo.forms.js

```
(function($, kendo) {
  var ui = kendo.ui,
    Widget = ui.Widget;

  var typeUpgrades = [
  {
    type: 'color',
    upgrade: function(inputs) {
      inputs.kendoColorPicker({ palette: 'basic' });
    }
  },
  {
    type: 'number',
```

```
  upgrade: function(inputs) {
    inputs.kendoNumericTextBox();
  }
},
{
  type: 'range',
  upgrade: function(inputs) {
    inputs.kendoSlider({
      showButtons: false,
      tickPlacement: 'none'
    });
  }
}];

var Form = Widget.extend({
  init: function(element, options) {
    var form = $(element),
      that = this;
    var i, len;

    // base call to widget initialization
    Widget.fn.init.call(this, element, options);

    function isFormTypeSupported(type) {
      if (type === 'text') { return true; }

      if (that.options.alwaysUseWidgets) {
        return false;
      }

      var input = document.createElement('input');
      input.setAttribute('type', type);
      return input.type !== 'text';
    }

    for (i = 0, len = typeUpgrades.length; i < len; i++) {
      var typeObj = typeUpgrades[i];

      if (!isFormTypeSupported(typeObj.type)) { ❶
        var inputs = form.find('input[type=' + typeObj.type + ']');
        typeObj.upgrade(inputs);
      }
    }
  },
  options: {
    // the name is what will appear in the kendo namespace (kendo.ui.Form).
    // The jQuery plug-in would be jQuery.fn.kendoForm.
    name: 'Form',
    alwaysUseWidgets: false
  }
});
```

```
    ui.plugin(Form);
} (jQuery, kendo));
```

❶   Test each feature before "upgrading"

In this snippet, I create an array called typeUpgrades to represent each form input type
and the "upgrade" logic needed to convert these into Kendo UI widgets. Then I create
a custom widget for my polyfill and specify the logic to perform when that widget is
initialized, which iterates over each type, finds any form fields that match, and finally,
upgrades each field based on its type.

The first perf tweak: caching feature tests

The preceding approach works, but perhaps you noticed that we perform the feature
detection test—creating an in-memory input element and setting its type—each and
every time. So, if I have 20 inputs on my form with the new color type, I'll perform this
dance 20 times. This is unnecessary. The user's browser won't change in the middle of
a page load, so there's really no reason for me to perform these feature tests each time
through. Instead, it makes more sense to test each feature when my library loads, and
cache the result of each test as a Boolean that I can access later. Example 5-2 shows an
example of this for my HTML5 Forms polyfill.

Example 5-2. Caching feature tests at first run in kendo.forms.js

```
(function($, kendo) {
  var ui = kendo.ui,
    Widget = ui.Widget;

  var typeUpgrades = [
  {
    type: 'color',
    upgrade: function(inputs) {
      inputs.kendoColorPicker({ palette: 'basic' });
    }
  },
  {
    type: 'number',
    upgrade: function(inputs) {
      inputs.kendoNumericTextBox();
    }
  },
  {
    type: 'range',
    upgrade: function(inputs) {
      inputs.kendoSlider({
        showButtons: false,
        tickPlacement: 'none'
      });
    }
  }];
```

```
function isFormTypeSupported(type) {
  var input = document.createElement('input');
  input.setAttribute('type', type);
  return input.type !== 'text';
}

var featureDetects = { ❶
  color: isFormTypeSupported('color'),
  number: isFormTypeSupported('number'),
  range: isFormTypeSupported('range')
};

var Form = Widget.extend({
  init: function(element, options) {
    var form = $(element),
      that = this;
    var i, len;

    // base call to widget initialization
    Widget.fn.init.call(this, element, options);

    for (i = 0, len = typeUpgrades.length; i < len; i++) {
      var typeObj = typeUpgrades[i];

      if (!featureDetects[typeObj.type] || that.alwaysUseWidgets) { ❷
        var inputs = form.find('input[type=' + typeObj.type + ']');
        typeObj.upgrade(inputs);
      }
    }
  },
  options: {
    // the name is what will appear in the kendo namespace (kendo.ui.Form).
    // The jQuery plug-in would be jQuery.fn.kendoForm.
    name: 'Form',
    alwaysUseWidgets: false
  }
});

ui.plugin(Form);
} (jQuery, kendo));
```

❶   Test and cache each feature test during the initial script load

❷   Access the cached test value during the "upgrade" process

In Example 5-2, I moved the isFormTypeSupported function outside my widget initialization code, and created a local featureDetects object to hold the cached Boolean values for each test. Finally, in my main initialization loop, I access those cached values, and bypass repeated code paths.

This is nice in theory, and it certainly looks a bit cleaner, but just how fast is it? To answer that question, I can head over to JSPerf (*http://jsperf.com*) and create a test.

Using JSPerf

JSPerf can seem a bit daunting if you've only ever viewed others' tests before, but it's actually quite simple to create tests of your own. The basic idea behind JSPerf is to create multiple test cases that execute blocks of JavaScript code—performing operations, mutating the DOM, and so forth—which the tool then executes over and over again in order to determine which operations are fastest and slowest. JSPerf takes care of all of the looping and reruns, so all you need to do is specify the test cases, and any setup or teardown that should happen before or after each test run.

In order to test just how much feature test caching improves the performance of our code, I created the test shown in Figure 5-1. You can also access the test online (*http://jsperf.com/feature-test-cache*), and run it yourself, if you so desire.

The "Preparation code" section in Figure 5-1 shows the setup and teardown code that will run before each test. This code does not impact the timing of the tests. Here, I create a global feature test method, `isFormTypeSupported`, as well as a global `featureDe tects` object, similar to Example 5-2.

The "Test Runner" section in Figure 5-1 contains my actual tests. The "Test Each Time" section does exactly what it says: each time that block is called, it will call the `isType Supported` method. This block mimics my original functionality in Example 5-1. The "Cache Tests" section in Figure 5-1, on the other hand, simply accesses the cached feature test values once. If I run these tests a few times, I'll get a result similar to Figure 5-2, which shows the test case from Figure 5-1 after I've run the test several times through in Chrome.

As you can see in Figure 5-2, caching my feature tests is not only faster, it's nearly 60 times faster on Chrome than performing feature tests each time! It's important to note that since JSPerf runs each test case several dozen times over, reported numbers aren't indicative of raw, overall performance gains in my library. Rather, JSPerf is most valuable as a measure of relative performance between options. I should also point out that performance gains—or losses—will vary from one browser to the next. In the preceding example, our gains in Chrome are far higher than IE, so it's important to test across browsers to get an accurate picture of changes. The bottom line, in this case, is that we know that caching feature tests is faster and thus an excellent refactoring choice for my library.

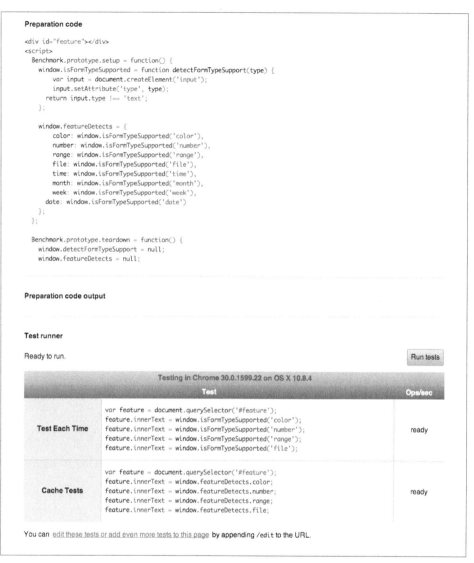

Figure 5-1. JSPerf test for feature test caching

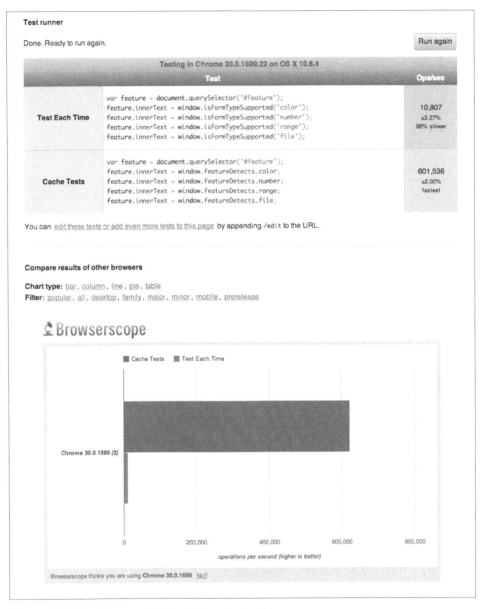

Figure 5-2. JSPerf test results for feature test caching

So far in this section, we've avoided executing unnecessary code by ensuring that feature-detection tests run only once when my library is loaded. Another important optimization I can perform is to ensure that my library doesn't perform any unnecessary initialization or setup. Any features or functionality that my library might not need for all browsers should remain dormant until it's needed. Obviously, stylesheets and JavaScript will need to be parsed when they are included, but I try to execute as little of that code as possible, until my library is called upon. In the case of my polyfill, the only code that runs before I initialize a form widget is my now cached feature tests, which I've deemed necessary to run up front since the performance gains are considerable.

3. Iterate Until You're Happy, Then Iterate Some More

The final strategy to keep your library performing well under the watchful eyes of consuming devs is to iterate, test, and iterate again. This is a bit of a hunt-and-peck exercise, where I look for micro- and macro-optimizations in my library, make changes, and then test those against the last version, using JSPerf. Some changes will make no difference in the performance of my library, while others will make a noticeable difference. Some might even harm performance, innocent as they may seem. The key is to code, test, iterate, and then test some more.

There's no science to this process, unfortunately, so I can't give you a bunch of tried-and-true tweaks that can be made to every library under the sun. I can, however, show you a couple of tweaks I made to my HTML5 Forms polyfill to give you an idea of what minor and major improvements might look like. Beyond these, your best bet is to pay attention to JavaScript best practices, as well as the proven practices of the libraries or frameworks you're utilizing. *Best practices* are often named as such because they promote maintenance, readability of code, and good performance, so you'll benefit from these even if they don't show considerable gains in your performance tests.

Before we proceed with the next few performance tweaks, I want to share the code samples for the complete HTML5 Forms polyfill. Thus far, I've included snippets only for three new input types. However, to properly show the impact of the next couple of refactors, we need to look at the complete source. In the production version of my polyfill, the source is broken into three modules, or files, that I concatenate during my build process. Those files are as follows:

kendo.forms.types.js
> Contains all of the input types supported by my polyfill, and the logic used to "upgrade" each to use a Kendo UI widget. The full source of this file can be viewed in Example 5-3.

kendo.forms.features.js
> Feature detection tests for my polyfill. The full source of this file can be viewed in Example 5-4.

kendo.forms.js
> The main source file for my polyfill. Contains widget initialization code and depends on *kendo.forms.types.js* and *kendo.forms.features.js*. The full source of this file can be viewed in Example 5-5.

Example 5-3. Contents of kendo.forms.types.js

```javascript
(function (kendo) {
  kendo.forms = kendo.forms || {};

  var typeUpgrades = [
  {
        type: 'color',
        upgrade: function(index, val) {
      $(val).kendoColorPicker({ palette: 'basic' });
    }
  },
  {
    type: 'number',
    upgrade: function(index, val) {
      $(val).kendoNumericTextBox();
    }
  },
  {
    type: 'range',
    upgrade: function(index, val) {
      $(val).kendoSlider({
        showButtons: false,
        tickPlacement: 'none'
      });
    }
  },
  {
    type: 'file',
    upgrade: function(index, val) {
      $(val).kendoUpload();
    }
  },
  {
    type: 'datetime',
    upgrade: dateTimeUpgrade
  },
  {
    type: 'datetime-local',
    upgrade: dateTimeUpgrade
  },
  {
    type: 'time',
    upgrade: function(index, val) {
      var input = $(val),
      dummyDate = '2013-10-04T';

      input.kendoTimePicker({
        value: input.val().length > 0 ? new Date(dummyDate + input.val())
          : null,
        min: input.attr('min') ? new Date(dummyDate + input.attr('min'))
          : new Date(2049, 0, 1, 0, 0, 0),
        max: input.attr('max') ? new Date(dummyDate + input.attr('max'))
```

```
          : new Date(2099, 11, 31, 0, 0, 0),
        // Step attribute is seconds, interval in minute
        interval: input.attr('step') ?
          Math.round(parseInt(input.attr('step'), 10)/60) : 30
      });
    }
},
        {
    type: 'month',
    upgrade: function(index, val) {
      var input = $(val),
        value = convertMonthPartToDate(input.val()),
        min = convertMonthPartToDate(input.attr('min')),
        max = convertMonthPartToDate(input.attr('max'));

      input.kendoDatePicker({
        // Set the start and depth properties to year, which means
        // that only month values are displayed.
        start: 'year',
        depth: 'year',
        // If the conversion returned a NaN, use the default values
        value: isNaN(value) ? null : new Date(value),
        min: isNaN(min) ? new Date(1900, 0, 1) : new Date(min),
        max: isNaN(max) ? new Date(2099, 11, 31) : new Date(max)
      });
    }
},
{
    type: 'week',
    upgrade: function(index, val) {
      var input = $(val),
        value = getDateFromWeekString(input.val()),
        min = getDateFromWeekString(input.attr('min')),
        max = getDateFromWeekString(input.attr('max'));

      input.kendoDatePicker({
        // Set the start and depth properties to month, which means
        // that only day/week values are displayed.
        depth: 'month',
        // If the conversion returned a null date, use the default values
        value: value,
        min: min === null ? new Date(1900, 0, 1) : min,
        max: max === null ? new Date(2099, 11, 31) : max
      });
    }
},
{
    type: 'date',
    upgrade: function(index, val) {
      var input = $(val);
      var defaults = getDateTimeDefaults(input);
      input.kendoDatePicker(defaults);
```

```
    }
}];

function convertMonthPartToDate(val) {
  // Add dummy day of month for valid date parsing
  val = val + '-' + new Date().getDate();
  return Date.parse(val);
}

function getDateFromWeekString(weekString) {
  var week, year,
    dateParts = weekString.split('-');

  if (dateParts.length < 2) {
    return null;
  }

  year = dateParts[0];
  week = dateParts[1].replace(/w/gi, '');

  if (isNaN(parseInt(week, 10)) || isNaN(parseInt(year, 10))) {
    return null;
  }

  // Jan 1 + 7 days per week
  var day = (1 + (week - 1) * 7);
  return new Date(year, 0, day);
}

function dateTimeUpgrade(index, val) {
  var input = $(val);

  // Step attribute is seconds, interval in minute
  var defaults = getDateTimeDefaults(input);
  defaults.interval = input.attr('step') ?
    Math.round(parseInt(input.attr('step'), 10)/60) : 30;
  input.kendoDateTimePicker(defaults);
}

function getDateTimeDefaults(input) {
  return {
    value: input.val().length > 0 ? new Date(input.val()) : null,
    min: input.attr('min') ? new Date(input.attr('min'))
      : new Date(1900, 0, 1),
    max: input.attr('max') ? new Date(input.attr('max'))
      : new Date(2099, 11, 31)
  };
}

kendo.forms.types = typeUpgrades;
} (kendo));
```

Example 5-4. Contents of kendo.forms.features.js

```javascript
(function (kendo) {
  kendo.forms = kendo.forms || {};

  function detectFormTypeSupport(type) {
    var input = document.createElement('input');
    input.setAttribute('type', type);
    return input.type !== 'text';
  }

  function detectDateTimeFields(type) {
    var dummyVal = ':(';

    var i = document.createElement('input');
    i.setAttribute('type', type);
    // Credit to Mike Taylor //gist.github.com/miketaylr/310734
    i.value = dummyVal;
    return (i.value !== dummyVal);
  }

  var featureDetects = {
    color: detectFormTypeSupport('color'),
    number: detectFormTypeSupport('number'),
    range: detectFormTypeSupport('range'),
    file: detectFormTypeSupport('file'),
    datetime: detectDateTimeFields('datetime'),
    datetime_local: detectFormTypeSupport('datetime-local'),
    time: detectFormTypeSupport('time'),
    month: detectFormTypeSupport('month'),
    week: detectFormTypeSupport('week'),
    date: detectFormTypeSupport('date'),
    placeholder: (function() {
      return 'placeholder' in document.createElement('input') &&
        'placeholder' in document.createElement('textarea');
    }())
  };

  kendo.forms.features = featureDetects;
} (kendo));
```

Example 5-5. Contents of kendo.forms.js

```javascript
(function($, kendo) {
  var ui = kendo.ui,
    Widget = ui.Widget,
    typeUpgrades = kendo.forms.types;

  var Form = Widget.extend({
    init: function(element, options) {
      var that = this;
      var form = $(element);
      var i, len;
```

```javascript
    var upgradeFormType = function(type, callback) {
      var modType = type.replace(/-/g,'_');

      if (!kendo.forms.features[modType] ||that.options.alwaysUseWidgets) {
        form.find('input[type=' + type + ']').each(callback);
      }
    };

    // base call to widget initialization
    Widget.fn.init.call(this, element, options);

    if (that.options.styleInputs) {
      form.find('input, button').each(function(index, val) {
      // Add the k-input class to each form element (or
      // k-button for buttons), providing Kendo UI styling
      // to all elements, not just those the widget will transform.
      var el = $(val);

      if (val.type === 'button' ||
        val.type === 'submit' ||
        val.type === 'reset') {
          el.addClass('k-button');
      } else {
        el.addClass('k-input');
      }
    });
  }

  // Add basic support for form types defined in the typeUpgrades array
  for (i = 0, len = typeUpgrades.length; i < len; i++) {
    var typeObj = typeUpgrades[i];
    upgradeFormType(typeObj.type, typeObj.upgrade);
  }

  // Add placeholder support if not provided by the browser
  if(!kendo.forms.features.placeholder) {
    form.find('[placeholder]').each(function(index, val) {
      var el = $(val);
      // Strip CR and LF from attribute vales, as specified in
      // www.w3.org/TR/html5/forms.html#the-placeholder-attribute
      var placeholderText = el.attr('placeholder')
        .replace(/(\\r\\n|\\n|\\r)/gm,'');

      // When the field loses focus, clear out the placeholder if
      // the input contains a value.
      el.on('blur', function() {
        var $el = $(this);
        var labelNode = this.previousSibling;
        if (this.value) {
          labelNode.nodeValue = '';
          $el.addClass('relPlaceholder');
```

```
        } else if (labelNode.nodeValue !== placeholderText) {
          labelNode.nodeValue = placeholderText;
          $el.removeClass('relPlaceholder');
        }
      });
      el.wrap('<label class="placeholder">' + placeholderText + '</label>');
      el.addClass('placeholder');
    });
  }
},

options: {
  // The name is what will appear in the kendo namespace (kendo.ui.Form).
  // The jQuery plug-in would be jQuery.fn.kendoForm.
  name: 'Form',
  alwaysUseWidgets: false,
  styleInputs: true
  }
});

ui.plugin(Form);
} (jQuery, kendo));
```

As we go through the next three performance tweaks, we'll make minor and major changes to the preceding sources. Once we're done with all three, I'll create another JSPerf test to compare each change so that we can measure the relative impact to performance. Let's take a look, first, at an easy change.

The second perf tweak: caching DOM elements

As you probably know, accessing and mutating the DOM is one of the most expensive operations you can make in JavaScript. Whether you're using a library like jQuery or a raw DOM selector method, such as `getElementById` or `querySelector`, selecting elements from your page is a memory-hogging, thread-blocking process that you want to perform with caution. This is not to say, of course, that you should *avoid* interacting with the DOM, because that would be silly. Rather, you should keep this reality in mind as you build your polyfills and do your best to minimize DOM interactions as much as possible.

While there are many ways to minimize DOM interactions in our JavaScript apps and polyfills, the two most common best practices are as follows:

- Minimize DOM reads by caching the result of selection operations into local variables.
- Minimize DOM writes by batching mutation operations together.

As an example of the batching approach, let's assume that I'm iterating over some collection of values in JavaScript and building up an HTML list (`<ul>` or `<li>`). Instead of appending each row (`<li>`) to my list, one at a time, a batching approach would lead me to build up the entire list in a string or DOM `DocumentFragment` and append the entire collection to the list container a single time. With this approach, I'm mutating the DOM—and triggering the browser's expensive layout, paint, and render operations —a single time, instead of once for each list item.

Chances are, if you've been doing frontend work for a while, this approach isn't news to you. We know that DOM writes are slow, and we take necessary precautions to avoid them. DOM reads, on the other hand, are a bit less worrisome, but still worth minimizing. As such, we address these by creating local variables for the result of DOM reads and operate on these variables when we need to access page elements.

An example of this element-caching approach with jQuery can be seen in Example 5-5. On line 10, you'll see the following:

```
var form = $(element);
```

In this case, `element` represents the `<form>` that I'm calling the Kendo UI widget constructor on (`new kendoForm()`). The jQuery method gives me the `<form>` element, which I then assign to the `form` variable.

Further down the sample, you'll notice that I then access this variable three additional times, each time calling `form.find` to further refine the list. In this case, even though the form itself is cached, jQuery has to return to the DOM to give me the collection of elements that match my `find` selector. Since all of my `find` operations are meant to operate on HTML input elements, I can make my cached variable a bit more targeted, which I've done in Example 5-6. Note that I've clipped some code from the source that's not relevant to the current discussion.

Example 5-6. kendo.forms.js polyfill main logic refactored to cache form inputs

```
(function($, kendo) {
  var ui = kendo.ui,
    Widget = ui.Widget,
    typeUpgrades = kendo.forms.types;

  var Form = Widget.extend({
    init: function(element, options) {
      var that = this;
      var inputs = $(element).find('input, button'); ❶
      var i, len;

      var upgradeFormType = function(type, callback) {
        // replace dash with underscore for features object lookup
        var modType = type.replace(/-/g,'_');

        if (!kendo.forms.features[modType] || that.options.alwaysUseWidgets) {
          inputs.filter('input[type=' + type + ']').each(callback); ❷
        }
```

```
    };

    // base call to widget initialization
    Widget.fn.init.call(this, element, options);

    if (that.options.styleInputs) {
      inputs.each(function(index, val) { ❸
        /* clipped */
      });
    }

    for (i = 0, len = typeUpgrades.length; i < len; i++) {
      var typeObj = typeUpgrades[i];
      upgradeFormType(typeObj.type, typeObj.upgrade);
    }

    // Add placeholder support if not provided by the browser
    if(!kendo.forms.features.placeholder) {
      /* clipped */
    }
  },

  options: { /* clipped */ }
});

ui.plugin(Form);
} (jQuery, kendo));
```

❶   Cache the collection of `<input>` and `<button>` elements in my form

❷   Use jQuery's `filter` method to get only the inputs that match the current type

❸   No need to filter here since the full collection is already cached.

Instead of caching the entire form in a local variable, I cache all of the `<input>` and `<button>` elements, since those are the only parts of the form I'm interested in at this point. With that new collection in hand, I'll use jQuery's `filter` method to refine the collection when I'm operating on a smaller subset. It's a small change, but it cleans up the DOM reads for my polyfill and makes things a bit more readable to boot. Now, before we test the performance impact of this change, let's make a few more tweaks so that we can view everything side by side at once.

The third perf tweak: ordering of arguments

The next change I'm going to make is a very small one, but it harkens back to the idea of avoiding unnecessary code paths as a way to get micro-optimizations in our code. Many times, these unneeded paths can be found in `if` statements that access one or more values before taking action. In Example 5-5, you'll notice the following `if` statement on line 17:

```
if (!kendo.forms.features[modType] || that.options.alwaysUseWidgets)
```

This statement determines whether the current input type (number) is supported by the user's browser *or* if the developer passed the alwaysUseWidgets option into the widget constructor. If either is true, we upgrade all instances of that input type on the form.

When dealing with multiconditioned if statements, it's always a good idea to consider how the order of arguments affects code execution. For instance, since the feature tests appear first, these will always be evaluated. If, however, I reorder these arguments, I can ensure that my feature test object will be accessed only if alwaysUseWidgets is false:

```
if (that.options.alwaysUseWidgets || !kendo.forms.features[modType])
```

Had I not already refactored my feature tests to run once during script evaluation, this would likely be a noticeable performance gain. As it stands now, each feature is returning a simple Boolean, so I don't expect to see much difference. Even still, I'm making this change to "future proof" my polyfill a bit. The alwaysUseWidgets option will always be a simple Boolean, but my feature tests could grow and become more complex as my library matures. Making this change now will keep me from introducing unintended performance costs down the road.

While the preceding example is a simple case for ordering arguments, it's always a good idea to order your simple Booleans first in your if statements. When performing an or (||) evaluation, this will ensure that the right-hand arguments aren't assessed unless the simple Boolean is false. When performing an and (&&) evaluation, right-hand arguments aren't assessed unless the simple Boolean is true. In both cases, your more complex method-call Booleans won't be evaluated unless their values are needed to fulfill or reject the condition in question.

The fourth perf tweak: minimizing loops

The final performance change I plan to make to my polyfill is a larger one, and is also a change that I expect to impact performance quite a bit. If you take a look at Example 5-5 a final time, you'll notice that I'm looping (with for or jQuery's each method) no less than four times during widget initialization. This can't be the best approach, so I'm going to refactor my polyfill to loop as infrequently as possible.

In Example 5-5, I'm looping over the typeUpgrades collection defined in ken do.forms.types, and then separately looping over each input that matches that type. What's more, I'm looping over each input to determine whether it needs separate widget styling (provided via CSS classes that Kendo UI uses to style "vanilla" inputs) and, finally, looping over each element that contains a placeholder attribute and upgrading those as well, if not supported by the browser.

As we built up our polyfill in Chapter 3, each of these additions made sense, and they do fulfill the functional requirements of my library. And yet, it all seems so inefficient.

This inefficiency was likely introduced as a result of my initial decision to loop first over input types and second over elements. At the time, this made sense because it allowed me to simultaneously upgrade all of the color, number, or datetime inputs on the form using jQuery's each method. But as I add other features, it becomes clear that my library will need to operate on each input individually, upgrading its type, dealing with attribute support, and even adding validation after I expand my library with that functionality.

So, to shift from several loops to a single loop, I need to move a few things around. For starters, my kendo.forms.types object needs to change. As illustrated in Example 5-7, I've changed the object from an array of type objects to a single object of key-value pairs. This will make it much easier for me to work with each type. You'll also notice that I moved some of the "upgrade" logic for vanilla inputs and buttons out of my main file and into this object as well.

Example 5-7. Refactored kendo.forms.types source

```
(function (kendo) {
  kendo.forms = kendo.forms || {};

  var typeUpgrades = {
    text: function(val) {
      $(val).addClass('k-input');
    },

    color: function(val) {
      $(val).kendoColorPicker({ palette: 'basic' });
    },

    number: function(val) {
      $(val).kendoNumericTextBox();
    },

    range: function(val) {
      $(val).kendoSlider({
        showButtons: false,
        tickPlacement: 'none'
      });
    },

    file: function(val) {
      $(val).kendoUpload();
    },

    /* clipped */
  };

  /* clipped */

  kendo.forms.types = typeUpgrades;
} (kendo));
```

Next, I'll make some changes to the core widget logic for my polyfill, as illustrated in Example 5-8. Not only have I collapsed things down into a single loop (in `puts.each()`), but I've also cleaned up my `init` method and moved some of the core logic into helper methods (`shouldUpgradeType`, `upgradeInputType`, `upgradePlace holder`).

Example 5-8. kendo.forms.js refactored to use a single loop

```
(function($, kendo) {
  var ui = kendo.ui,
    Widget = ui.Widget,
    typeUpgrades = kendo.forms.types,
    features = kendo.forms.features,
    vanillaInputRegEx = /text|button|submit|reset/i;

  var Form = Widget.extend({
    init: function(element, options) {
      var that = this;
      var inputs = $(element).find('input, button');

      Widget.fn.init.call(this, element, options);

      inputs.each(function(index, el) {   ❶
        that.upgradeInputType(that, el);   ❷

        if (el.getAttribute('placeholder') &&
          !kendo.forms.features.placeholder) {
          that.upgradePlaceholder(el);   ❸
        }
      });
    },
    shouldUpgradeType: function(type) {
      /* clipped */
    },
    upgradeInputType: function(that, el) {
      var type = el.getAttribute('type');

      if (!type && el.nodeName === 'BUTTON') {
        type = 'button';
      }

      if(vanillaInputRegEx.test(type) && that.options.styleInputs) {
        typeUpgrades[type](el);
      }

      if (that.shouldUpgradeType(type)) {
        typeUpgrades[type](el);
      }
    },
    upgradePlaceholder: function(el) {
      /* clipped */
```

```
    },
    options: {
      name: 'Form',
      alwaysUseWidgets: false,
      styleInputs: true
    }
  });

  ui.plugin(Form);
} (jQuery, kendo));
```

❶   Single loop for evaluating all form inputs

❷   Core upgrade functionality, refactored into an external function

❸   Upgrade functionality for the placeholder attribute, refactored into an external
    function

I think you'll agree that this is much cleaner, but is it any faster? For that matter, have
any of these changes made a difference? Let's take a look in the next section.

Running Performance Benchmarks

One of the nice things about JSPerf is that, with a little bit of setup, it's easy to do side-
by-side testing of revisions to your code. Along those lines, I created a new JSPerf test
that includes all of the tweaks we've made in this chapter, and you can view it online
(*http://bit.ly/jsperftest*). You can also append /edit to the end of the URL if you want
to see how the test was set up, or make edits of your own.

For this test, I included the same sample form that we created in Chapter 3, and used
JSPerf's setup capability to load a different version of my polyfill source, depending on
the individual test case. All told, I created four tests:

- A baseline test, before any changes were made
- A test for the element-caching refactor
- A test of the argument-ordering refactor
- A test for the single loop refactor

The results can be seen in Figure 5-3. The results for an individual run can be seen in
the top part of the image, with summary results for all browsers at the bottom. There
are a couple of things to take away from this image:

1. Individual test runs can give different results, so be sure to run your tests several
   times, and in as many browsers as possible. In the last image, my element-cache
   refactor looks like the slowest test, though it's still well within the standard deviation
   (+/-) of 4.96% indicated by JSPerf. If you look at the bar charts at the bottom of the

image, you'll note that, over a larger sample size, the element-cache refactor (in yellow) is faster than my baseline test (in red) in most browsers.

2. For most browsers, the argument-reordering change isn't much faster than the element-cache refactor. I expected this; so as long as it's not noticeably *slower*, it's a worthwhile change. However, it does seem to be visibly faster in the current version of Chrome (at the time of writing), so I'll take it.

3. Finally, as expected, the single-loop refactor yielded the largest gains across most browsers, especially Chrome. It's faster in Opera and Safari, though because of the huge speed improvements in modern browsers, the IE8 row looks empty. Surprisingly, these changes are all about even on Firefox but, again, since performance isn't markedly worse, I'm OK with an outlier or two.

Tune It But Don't Overdo It

As I have mentioned before, there's not really much science involved in making performance tweaks to your polyfill. It's more an exercise of trial and error with the goal of finding micro- and macro-optimizations that make your library faster. In the preceding examples, I made some small and large changes based on my knowledge of good JavaScript practices, and it turned out that those changes yielded some gains in most browsers.

Before I close this section, a word of caution: performance tuning is important, and it's something you should spend time on, but I suggest being careful with it. It's easy to make common sense changes that you might have missed in initial development, but once you've made a handful of obvious or even non-obvious tweaks, diminishing returns will start to set in, and you'll be spending far too much time making changes to eke out an extra tenth of a percent speed improvement. When it starts to feel like each change isn't moving the performance needle enough, or even moving it in the wrong direction, it's time to feel confident that you've done your best, and move on.

Dealing with Browser-Specific Edge Cases

Now that we've talked about general performance testing, I'll close this chapter with a brief discussion about browser-specific edge cases. As you can see from the previous sections, it's possible to set up a very robust process for testing performance across several browsers. This is useful, but there will always be outliers in both performance and functionality (in our case, IE7 and 8). Once we've identified these, it's time to investigate with some additional, manual tests.

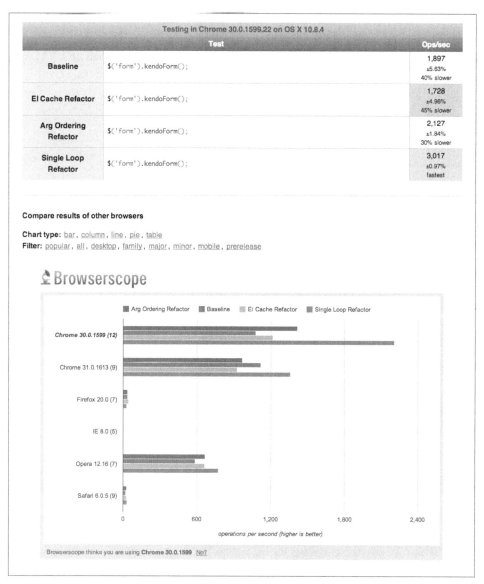

Testing in Chrome 30.0.1599.22 on OS X 10.8.4		
Test		**Ops/sec**
Baseline	`$('form').kendoForm();`	1,897 ±5.63% 40% slower
El Cache Refactor	`$('form').kendoForm();`	1,728 ±4.96% 45% slower
Arg Ordering Refactor	`$('form').kendoForm();`	2,127 ±1.84% 30% slower
Single Loop Refactor	`$('form').kendoForm();`	3,017 ±0.97% fastest

Compare results of other browsers

Chart type: bar, column, line, pie, table
Filter: popular, all, desktop, family, major, minor, mobile, prerelease

Figure 5-3. JSPerf test for tweaks 2–4

Regardless of your build and automated testing workflow, there's no substitute for hands-on actual testing with certain browsers, especially oldIE. While it's still important to test IE7 and 8 for most kinds of sites and apps, it's critically important when you are building polyfills. More often than not, IE7 and 8 will need the functionality your polyfill provides, so you'll want to test on these browsers early and often.

After making each of the performance tweaks listed in this chapter, I was sure to run all of my automated tests with the `grunt test` and `grunt x-test` commands I set up in Chapter 4. Everything looks great in the latest browsers, but when I open up a VM with IE8 or IE7, I see something that looks more like Figure 5-4.

Figure 5-4. Testing my polyfill with IE8

In spite of all of my testing, I still have a handful of failing tests in IE7 and 8. Digging deeper, however, I see that they're all date- and time-related tests, which suggests a common cause for all of these. Let's take a look at the first failing test, which is listed in Example 5-9.

Example 5-9. DateTime Jasmine test block in fixtures.js

```javascript
describe('DateTime and datetime-local type Support', function() {
  it('should apply the datetime attributes (val, min, max, step) to the widget',
    function() {
    fixtures.load('datetime-type.html');

    $('#datetime-form').kendoForm();

    var datetimeInput = $('#datetime');
    var datetimeObject = datetimeInput.data('kendoDateTimePicker');

    var dateRegex = /\/|-| /g;
    var valParts = datetimeInput.val().split(dateRegex);
    var minParts = datetimeInput.attr('min').split(dateRegex);
    var maxParts = datetimeInput.attr('max').split(dateRegex);

    expect(datetimeObject.value()).not.toBeNull();
    expect(datetimeObject.value().getMonth()+1).toEqual(
      parseInt(valParts[0], 10));  ❶
    expect(datetimeObject.value().getDate()).toEqual(
      parseInt(valParts[1], 10));

    expect(datetimeObject.value().getFullYear()).toEqual(
      parseInt(valParts[2], 10));

    // Run Same tests for min and max date values
    // ...
  });
}
```

❶   This test fails here in IE7 and 8

This test, which I've clipped for readability, is designed to make sure that the Kendo UI DateTime widget is properly initialized with the date input's `value` attribute. In IE7 and 8, this test fails at the second `expect`. Upon further investigation, it appears that the `dateTimeObject` variable is null because my DateTime widget wasn't properly initialized. That means that the problem is in my "upgrade" function, which I've included in Example 5-10.

Example 5-10. DateTime upgrade logic added to kendo.forms.features.js

```javascript
var typeUpgrades = {
  datetime: function (val) {
    var input = $(val);

    // Step attribute is seconds, interval in minute
    var defaults = getDateTimeDefaults(input);
    defaults.interval = input.attr('step') ?
      Math.round(parseInt(input.attr('step'), 10)/60) : 30;
    input.kendoDateTimePicker(defaults);
```

```
  }
  /* Other upgrades */
};

function getDateTimeDefaults(input) {
  return {
    value: input.val().length > 0 ? new Date(input.val()) : null,
    min: input.attr('min') ? new Date(input.attr('min'))
      : new Date(1900, 0, 1),
    max: input.attr('max') ? new Date(input.attr('max'))
      : new Date(2099, 11, 31)
  };
}

kendo.forms.types = typeUpgrades;
```

The issue, it would seem, is with the `getDateTimeDefaults` helper function, which takes my input and returns an object with date values that I then pass to the Kendo UI `kendoDateTimePicker` method. If you look closely, you'll notice that I'm not properly sanitizing my attribute values to make sure that they contain a valid date. Instead, I'm merely checking for the presence of any value before calling the `new Date()` constructor on that value. Even still, these are my own unit tests, and I'm passing only perfectly valid ISO date strings, as per the forms section of the HTML5 spec, so why in the world are my tests failing?

The answer is deceptively simple: IE7 and 8 don't support the ISO Date standard when parsing date strings. Welcome to the world of cross-browser polyfill development, my friends! Thankfully, it's a relatively simple fix. If I wanted to take an external dependency, I could include a library like Moment.js (*http://moment.js*) to handle the hassle of date parsing. I can also leverage built-in features of Kendo UI or jQuery to help. For the sake of completeness, however, in this case, I'm going to add my own fix. First, I'll add a new `createDateFromInput` method to the *kendo.forms.types.js* file, as shown in Example 5-11.

Example 5-11. Handling ISO and non-ISO date formats for oldIE in kend.forms.features.js

```
function createDateFromInput(val, defaultDate, prefix) {
  if (!val) { return defaultDate; }

  if (prefix) { val = prefix + val; }

  if (!Date.parse(val)) {
    // Valid ISO Dates may not parse on some browsers (IE7,8)
    var altDate = new Date(val.replace(/-/g, '/'));

    if (altDate) {
      // If this alternate value is valid, add a day
      // to account for UA parsing
```

```
    return new Date(altDate.setDate(altDate.getDate() + 1));
  }

  return defaultDate;
}

return new Date(val);
}
```

This simplistic solution takes a string value, a defaultDate, and an optional prefix value, which I'll need to parse the HTML5 time and month input types. If the passed-in value parses correctly, I'll return a new Date object with that value. If not, I'll replace the dashes (-) with slashes (/) and attempt to parse again, which should resolve my issues in IE7 and 8.

Next, I can modify my getDateTimeDefaults function to use this new function:

```
function getDateTimeDefaults(input) {
  return {
    value: createDateFromInput(input.val(), null),
    min: createDateFromInput(input.attr('min'), new Date(1900, 0, 1)),
    max: createDateFromInput(input.attr('max'), new Date(2099, 11, 31))
  };
}
```

With this in place, my datetime and datetime-local tests will pass. The remaining failing tests relate to similar problems with the time and month input types, and as soon as I modify those upgrade functions to use my new helper method, I should see all passing tests in IE7 and 8, as shown in Figure 5-5.

Much like performance testing, cross-browser issues are hard to generalize. Each browser has its own quirks and edge cases that behave differently from all the rest. IE7 and 8 certainly aren't alone in this regard. Modern specs have done a great job of minimizing these types of differences in newer browsers, but you should expect to encounter hairy issues from time to time as you build cross-browser polyfills. Thankfully, these quirks and their workarounds are often well documented, so you shouldn't need to go far to find a fix.

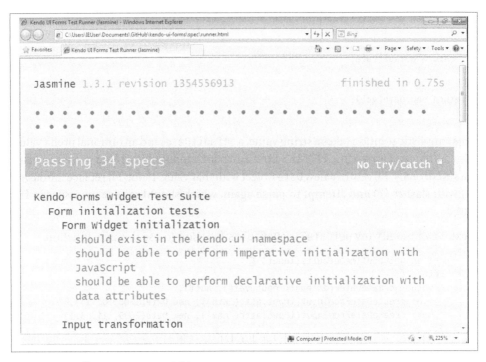

Figure 5-5. All tests passing in IE8

Mobile-Specific Considerations

In this chapter, we've focused mostly on overall JavaScript and DOM rendering performance considerations. While this is important for all browsers, you'll often find that you need to focus specifically on mobile for polyfills that are meant to be used on devices. In addition to the tips shared previously, let's look at a couple of mobile-specific performance recommendations:

- File size matters.
- Always test on devices.

File Size Matters

While also true for the desktop, it's critical that you pay attention to overall file size when building polyfills for mobile and devices. Not only does the size of a JavaScript or CSS file affect the rendering time on devices—which often have browser engines that don't perform as fast as their desktop counterparts—but a larger file means more bytes for the mobile device to download from the network, which has a cost on both the user's battery and data plan.

Web developers are becoming increasingly aware of the performance impact on app resources, so do your fellow developers a favor and make sure that your polyfill is as small as possible, both by including only the needed functionality and also by delivering a minified production version of your library. If your polyfill is broad in scope, as is the case of the HTML5 Forms Library, you might even consider providing functionality in modules that can be delivered separately or combined via a custom build process.

In the case of our Forms polyfill, it's also important for me to think about the file size of my dependencies. Specifically, in the case of Kendo UI Web, I'm using only a subset of all of the widgets and features available in this library, so it doesn't make sense to require the end user to download that entire file. Thankfully, Kendo UI provides its widgets in a modular form, and I can use these to create a custom build of the library that uses only the widgets required, and then ship this with the source of my polyfill.

Always Test on Devices

Perhaps it goes without saying, but in today's mobile world, testing across browsers means testing device browsers, too. And even though the device browsers are mobile versions of their desktop counterparts, it doesn't mean that every feature available in Chrome for the desktop is also available in Chrome for mobile. What's more, because the speed and performance of your library is just as important as its functionality, it's critical that you regularly run your tests on physical mobile devices to ensure that you're delivering a great polyfill experience.

Unfortunately, it's not possible to use Karma to automatically test mobile browsers—BrowserStack does have mobile emulators, but it's a paid product—so you'll likely need to rely on friends, family, and the goodwill of developers working with your polyfill to test across devices. Even better, if you live in a city with an open device lab, consider scheduling regular visits for testing. Finally, there are paid services—for example, DeviceAnywhere—for accessing physical devices for testing, but since you're not likely to be building your polyfill for profit, it's probably not worth the steep cost of these services.

Over the last three chapters, we've discussed many of the ins and outs of building your own cross-browser polyfills. In Chapter 3, we explored some practices for project structure and explored the ins and outs of adding initial functionality and a bit of refactoring. Then, in Chapter 4, we configured a solid build and test environment that allowed us to test our polyfill in the browser and via command-line tools like Grunt, Jasmine, and Karma. Finally, we looked at performance and edge-case tuning, and explored some examples using JSPerf to fine-tune the speed of our polyfill. Collectively, you should have a solid foundation to use for building your own polyfills, and I can't wait to see what you'll come up with!

Next, we'll turn the discussion to future polyfilling, or the practice of adding new APIs and functionality to our browsers, for the purpose of vetting and testing out what's next for the web platform.

Prollyfilling and the Future of the Web Platform

In Part I, we looked at polyfilling in its original context: a strategy for "filling in the gaps" of older browsers with modern web APIs and technologies. In Part II, we'll shift our focus from the past and present and look toward the future. Specifically, we'll talk about a variation of polyfilling that enables developers to experiment with not-yet-standardized APIs and developer-driven ideas that could make their way into the browsers in the future. In Chapter 6, I'll introduce the future of polyfilling, the prollyfill, and will provide several examples of popular and notable prollyfilling libraries that push the boundaries of the web platform. Then, in Chapter 7, I'll close this book with a hands-on exploration of prollyfill construction, and how it compares to our polyfill construction exercise in Part I.

The Future of Polyfilling

As our browsers release updates at a faster and faster clip, and legacy browsers like IE6–8 decline in global use, it's easy to fall into the trap of thinking that polyfilling, as an idea, is becoming increasingly irrelevant. And while it's true that "classical" polyfills for popular HTML5 and CSS3 features are being used less and less, for every mainstream feature in the web platform, like CSS3 animations, we're seeing three or four new ideas and technologies introduced via the W3C or WHATWG and landing in one or more browsers. HTML5 and friends may have modernized the Web and our browsers in key ways, but don't think for a moment that they also brought feature parity along for the ride.

Polyfilling: Not Just For Older Browsers

The bottom line is this: each new feature that's supported in Firefox but has yet to be implemented in Chrome, IE, or Safari needs a polyfill just as much as that local storage feature you'd like to offer to IE7 users. If newer technologies are to take off and become accepted by developers, we need to use them on actual sites. In some cases, we might take a *forked experience* approach and support the feature only where native to the browser. In many cases, however, new features bring capabilities that we wish to share with as many of our users as possible. In this case, pollyfilling is a must.

Prollyfilling: Extending the Web Forward

Sometimes, pollyfilling specified features isn't always enough for us, as web developers. We're a smart, ambitious bunch, and this is our platform too. Most of the time, we think we're just as qualified as browser vendors when it comes to determining what capabilities the web platform, and our browsers, really need.

In Chapter 1, I mentioned something called the Extensible Web Manifesto (*http://bit.ly/ exwebman*), a rallying cry of sorts for frontend developers. It's one that calls us to "extend the Web forward" by working on speculative and cutting-edge ideas in our browsers. It also calls upon browser vendors to unlock low-level capabilities in the browser (for instance, the browser's networking stack or its HTML parser) and allow developers to write their own JavaScript libraries and APIs on top of those capabilities. The core idea that the manifesto argues for is that, with access to these low-level APIs, developers can experiment with real-world ideas that solve real-world problems. I use the term *real-world* here, because, on occasion, the W3C will pursue ideas that, while academically sound, are rejected by developers when subjected to actual use.

Take the oft-maligned Application Cache, for instance. This specification, which enjoys wide support across all modern desktop and mobile browsers, was introduced as a declarative API intended to solve the very real problem of caching websites and applications for offline use. It's a fantastic idea, and developers everywhere applauded the introduction of the technology when it was first introduced several years ago.

But the honeymoon hasn't lasted. After being subjected to real-world use on sites and applications of all sizes, developers discovered that AppCache is plagued by a series of bugs and bug-like features that make the technology difficult or sometimes impossible to rely on. Ironically, while the Application Cache seems well suited for content-driven and static sites, it is weakest when used for dynamic web-based applications.

If the authors and advocates of the Extensible Web Manifesto have their way, new technologies like Application Cache would not be introduced for full-blown standardization without first spending some time in the hands of developers. And by unlocking certain low-level browser APIs, like those mentioned previously, developers can not only vet new ideas, but can also be a source of new ideas and feature proposals.

At its core, this idea is referred to as *forward polyfilling*, or *prollyfilling*, the latter term being half-jokingly coined by Alex Sexton to describe building a polyfill for a not-yet-standardized API (ostensibly, this term is a mixture of "probably" and "polyfill"). Prollyfilling builds on the core ideas of polyfilling, building cross-browser functionality on which developers can rely, but places it square in the mix of the standardization process, which I believe will make the practice critical to the success of the web platform over the next decade.

Prollyfills In Action: Prollyfilling CSS

So what does a prollyfill look like? It varies, and sometimes pretty widely. There are prollyfills in use today that not only provide experimental JavaScript APIs to developers, but also allow developers to author custom HTML or CSS. We'll look at examples of all three types of prollyfills in this chapter, starting with a library that allows developers to try out experimental CSS features, and even create some of our own.

If you're a CSS aficionado, you know that there are some great new features on the horizon, like filter effects, grid layout, regions, exclusions, and more. Another exciting set of enhancements are being proposed in the CSS Selectors Level 4 specification (*http://*

bit.ly/selectors4), through which the CSS Working Group hopes to add a bevy of new, powerful selectors, while also upgrading some selectors introduced with CSS3.

For example, consider the new `:matches` pseudoclass selector. This selector allows developers to group matching elements with simpler syntax than is possible currently. For instance, consider the following:

```
ul.tasks li a:link,
ul.tasks li a:hover,
ul.tasks li a:visited,
ul.tasks li a:focus {
    color: blue;
}
```

With the new `:matches` pseudoclass selector, this rule could be shortened, like so:

```
ul.tasks li a:matches(:link, :hover, :visited, :focus) {
    color: blue;
}
```

It's a simple change, but it greatly cleans up the authoring experience, while also making your CSS just a bit more readable, which is nice. `:matches` is just one example of the great new CSS selectors in the Level 4 spec. The only problem is that we can't exactly try these experimental new selectors out for ourselves because they're still being discussed in the CSS Working Group and have not yet landed in any browser. But in the meantime, wouldn't it be great if we could actually start using new pseudoclass selectors like `:matches` and even try out a few of our own? And not just to be early adopters, but to really try these new features on for size and see if they work as designed.

Using HitchJS to Experiment with CSS

This sounds like a sweet spot for prollyfilling and, thankfully, there's a library available that allows you to experiment with CSS selectors and even define your own. The library is called HitchJS (*http://hitchjs.com*) because it allows you to "hitch new capabilities to the browser," according to its creator Brian Kardell. Out of the box, Hitch provides support for a series of experimental selectors like `oneof`, `anyof`, and `allof`, and also provides a mechanism that allows you to define your own *hitches* that activate whatever CSS selectors you define. We'll create our own hitch in the next section, but first, let's take a look at how you can get started with Hitch and use some of the built-in features.

First things first: you'll need to download Hitch, which is distributed as a script file, and then include a reference to the file anywhere in your page:

```
<script src="js/hitch-0.6.3.min.js"></script>
```

Next, you activate Hitch by decorating `<style>` and `<link>` tags with the `data-hitch-interpret` attribute, which tells Hitch to scan the CSS at the location for library-specific selectors:

```
<link rel="stylesheet" href="css/styles.css" data-hitch-interpret>
```

In this example, I'm telling Hitch to look for rules in the *styles.css* file. Example 6-1 contains the contents of that file.

Example 6-1. Custom CSS using HitchJS's built-in rules

```
#todo-list li:-hitch-anyof(.urgent, .overdue) label {
  color: red;
}

#todo-list li:-hitch-noneof(.urgent, .overdue) label {
  color: green;
}

#todo-list li:-hitch-allof(.urgent, .overdue) label {
  font-weight: bold;
}
```

Notice the pseudoclass selectors that start with -hitch-. All three of these, -hitch-anyof, -hitch-noneof, and -hitch-allof are selectors that Hitch provides out of the box. Anyof will match any element in the comma-delimited list; noneof is a negation selector that will apply the rule only if the li has none of the classes in the list; and allof is inclusive (only li elements with both classes will match and apply the rule).

Now let's take a look at the source HTML (in Example 6-2), which is a list of to-dos decorated with classes where the to-do is urgent, overdue, or both:

Example 6-2. To-do list HTML

```
<ul id="todo-list">
  <li class="">
    <div class="view">
      <input class="toggle" type="checkbox">
      <label>Take out the trash</label>
    </div>
  </li>
  <li class="">
    <div class="view">
      <input class="toggle" type="checkbox">
      <label>Wash the cars</label>
    </div>
  </li>
  <li class="overdue">
    <div class="view">
      <input class="toggle" type="checkbox">
      <label>Buy stamps</label>
    </div>
  </li>
  <li class="urgent overdue">
    <div class="view">
      <input class="toggle" type="checkbox">
```

```
      <label>Pay taxes</label>
    </div>
  </li>
  <li class="urgent" id="next-action">
    <div class="view">
      <input class="toggle" type="checkbox">
      <label>Catch up on Breaking Bad</label>
    </div>
  </li>
</ul>
```

With everything in place, I should be able to load my to-do list and see the additional styling that my Hitch-based rules provide, as illustrated in Figure 6-1.

Figure 6-1. To-do list with HitchJS-based styling

You might notice a flash of unstyled content as you load a page that uses Hitch.js features. Because Hitch processes custom CSS rules after the rest of the CSS in the document has been applied, this is to be expected. What's more, since we're testing ideas here and not building production apps with our prollyfills, I think we can live with this.

As you can see, HitchJS is easy to get started with and use in your own apps. By default, Hitch provides support for four logical selectors (`:-hitch-anyof`, `:-hitch-allof`, `:-hitch-oneof`, `:-hitch-noneof`) and one structural selector (`:-hitch-has`), but the library also provides a great extensibility story so that you can create your own selector support in the form of hitches that are imported and processed by HitchJS. In the next section, we'll create our own hitch to mimic a new CSS Selector.

Building Your Own Hitches

Earlier in this chapter, I introduced the new `:matches` pseudoclass selector being considered for inclusion in the Selectors Level 4 spec. Rather than waiting for one or more browsers to implement support for this new selector, I'd like to try it on for size in my own apps—and possibly even share my experiences with other developers and members of the CSS Working Group. HitchJS allows me to do this. I should probably note that, functionally, the `-hitch-anyof` selector is very similar to how `:matches` is specified. I'm building our own hitch, however, to adhere to the name and also experiment with my own implementations. With the library as a dependency, I can create a hitch, or a JavaScript module of my own that defines the logic for my selector. I then import that custom logic into my app, and when HitchJS is activated, it calls my module to determine whether the element in question matches my custom selector.

So, to define my custom hitch for the CSS `:matches` selector, I'll first need to create a new file called *selector-matches.js* in my project. Then, I'll add the initial module definition that Hitch requires, as illustrated in Example 6-3.

Example 6-3. Creating a hitch for the `matches` selector in selector-matches.js

```
var matchesHitch = {
  name: "matches",
  base: "*",
  type: "selector",
  filter: function(el, arguments){
    // Hitch logic here
  }
};
Hitch.add(matchesHitch);
```

The `matchesHitch` object contains all of the properties that HitchJS requires when I define my own hitches. Most important, the `name` represents the CSS selector value, and the `filter` represents a function that runs against every element that matches the base selector, but that needs to be filtered further by my hitch. This method should contain the core logic for my hitch and should return a Boolean after I determine whether the element in question meets the filter criteria.

To emulate the CSS Selectors Level 4 `:matches` pseudoclass selector, I'll need to test a comma-delimited string of `class` and `id` values against an element. If the element contains any of the values specified in the :matches selector, I'll return true, at which point Hitch will apply the CSS defined inside my custom selector. The source for my Hitch's filter method can be found in Example 6-4.

Example 6-4. Custom matches selector method in selector-matches.js

```
filter: function(el, selectorArgs){
  var i, len,
    match = false,
    args = selectorArgs.split(','),
    list = el.parentElement;

  for (i = 0, len = args.length; i < len; i++) {
    var q = list.querySelector(args[i].trim());

    if (q && q === el) {
      match = true;
    }
  }

  return match;
}
```

After setting up some helper variables, I split my selectorArgs variable, which contains the comma-delimited list of classes and ids into an array. Then, I loop over that array and attempt to match each selector argument against the current element. If the element has all of the values defined in the selectorArgs array, I'll return true, and the styles inside the :matches-dependent rule will be applied.

Now that we have our custom hitch, let's try out our new rule in CSS. First, I'll need to import my hitch by using Hitch's @-hitch-requires directive at the top of my *styles.css* file:

```
@-hitch-requires ../js/selector-matches.js;
```

Then, I'll add a new rule using my hitch:

```
#todo-list li:matches(.urgent, #next-action) label {
  font-weight: bold;
  color: blue;
}
```

With this rule, I'm instructing my custom hitch to look for any li with a class of urgent and an id of next-action, and to style the label for that li to be bold and have a blue color. And with that, we have prollyfill-based support for the CSS :matches rule, courtesy of HitchJS! The result can be seen in Figure 6-2. Note that the styles in the image are taken from the fantastic TodoMVC project (*http://todomvc.com*). If you're following along at home and want to emulate the same styles, you can grab them from any of the samples in the project website.

Figure 6-2. Our custom hitch in action

HitchJS is a versatile library, and now that you've seen how easy it is to create your own hitches, you've got everything you need to try our experimental CSS features, or even prototype and play with your own!

Prollyfills in Action: ServiceWorker

In the previous section, we explored how prollyfills can be useful for experimenting with new or unstable CSS selectors. Next, we'll shift focus to JavaScript prollyfilling. Specifically, we'll look at a proposal for one of those low-level APIs that could open up a wealth of new opportunities for frontend developers: ServiceWorker (*http://bit.ly/ servicework*).

ServiceWorker is a proposal, spearheaded by Alex Russell of Google and others, designed to make the browser's networking stack more programmable via JavaScript. Specifically, a ServiceWorker enables developers to use JavaScript to cache and handle every inbound request for resources in an app, even when the user is offline.

If you're thinking that this is starting to sound a lot like a JavaScript-based version of the oft-maligned Application Cache, you'd be right, and also wrong at the same time. Because ServiceWorker is meant to be a low-level API, it's far broader than an imperative

AppCache. It can certainly be used to handle application asset and resource caching, but it's also far broader than that. In a very general sense, a ServiceWorker is a script that, when installed in your app, listens for network events. When those events occur, a ServiceWorker can intercept the network request and serve cached resources before the browser ever attempts to connect to a remote server.

The first step in using a ServiceWorker is to install a worker on a page after a user visits for the first time. This means that the page, and all of its resources, will be served from the network at least once before the worker takes over. Example 6-5 shows an example of what the API for creating a new worker could look like.

 At the time of writing, ServiceWorker is not available in any browser. As such, the following snippets are not runnable.

Example 6-5. Creating a new ServiceWorker object

```html
<!DOCTYPE html>
<!-- http://www.gifsemporium.com/index.html -->
<html>
  <head>
    <link rel="stylesheet" href="/css/base.css">
    <script src="/js/app.js"></script>
        <script>
      navigator.registerServiceWorker("/*", "sWorker.js").then(
        function(serviceWorker) {
          // Use the worker right away
          window.location.reload();
        },
        function(err) {
          console.error("Worker install failed:", err);
        });
    </script>
  </head>
  <body>
    <img src="/images/logo.gif" alt="Gif Emporium Logo">
    <h1>Animated Gifs Galore!</h1>
  </body>
</html>
```

The key snippet here is the call to `navigator.registerServiceWorker`, which takes two parameters: a route or set of routes to handle with our ServiceWorker, and the path to a JavaScript file that contains the worker logic. The API is also promise-based, so I can call `then()` on the API with success and error handlers and notify the system of a successful or failed worker registration. A sample *sWorker.js* file can be found in Example 6-6.

Example 6-6. A sample ServiceWorker controller

```
// hosted at: js/sWorker.js

var base = "http://www.gifsemporium.com";
var inventory = new URL("/services/gifs.json", base);

this.addEventListener("install", function(e) {
  // this worker can handle fetch events
  e.services = ["fetch"];
});

this.addEventListener("fetch", function(e) {
  var url = e.request.url;

  // If we already have the data, load from cache
  if (url.toString() == inventory.toString()) {
    e.respondWith(new SameOriginResponse({
      statusCode: 200,
      body: JSON.stringify({
        gifs: { /* ... */ }
      })
    }));
  }
});
```

The ServiceWorker exposes several events that workers can respond to, if they wish. If a worker is installed and has registered a `fetch` listener, as we have in this example, the worker is allowed to handle the network request on behalf of the browser. In this case, we're checking to see whether the URL being requested matches an existing resource and, if so, we'll use the new `respondWith` method on the `fetch` event to construct a cached response containing the data requested by the browser, and the network never even needs to be consulted!

The public API for the ServiceWorker proposal can be found in a TypeScript file in the project's GitHub repository (*http://bit.ly/serviceworker*), and I also recommend checking out the explainer document (*http://bit.ly/serv-explainer*) put together by the people working on the proposal. ServiceWorker is still in its early days, so it doesn't yet enjoy browser support, but the proposal is exactly the kind of API described in the Extensible Web Manifesto: a set of low-level browser capabilities that provide developers with ground-floor access to building robust, JavaScript-based prollyfills and APIs that push the Web forward faster than ever.

Prollyfills in Action: Web Components

So far, we've looked at how prollyfills can help us work with experimental CSS and JavaScript, but what about experimenting with HTML itself? Before you laugh me out of town and put down the book, bear with me.

As it turns out, there are a handful of W3C specifications that have been in the making for the last few years that do just that: provide an official way for developers and site authors to extend the semantics of HTML for apps. These specifications are typically referred to using the umbrella term of *Web Components*. According to the W3C (*http:// bit.ly/web-comps*), "Web components enable web application authors to define widgets with a level of visual richness and interactivity not possible with CSS alone, and ease of composition and reuse not possible with script libraries today."

Widgets? Composition? Reuse? If you've been a developer for any length of time, these terms are familiar to you, but did you ever think you'd hear them in the context of HTML? Me neither, and yet here we are, talking about ways to bring a first-class widget construction workflow to the Web.

Web Components are made up of five key, standalone W3C specifications. One of these, Decorators (*http://bit.ly/w3-decor*) is the least relevant to our discussion and the most raw of the specs, so I'll skip it. Here's a brief summary of the other four.

Templates

Templates (*http://bit.ly/w3-templates*) are defined as "inert chunks of markup" that can be activated for use later. This spec will be the most familiar to developers because it essentially formalizes what we've long accomplished using <script> elements with a non-JavaScript type attribute. Example 6-7 shows a simple <template> element and the JavaScript activation code.

Example 6-7. An example use of the <template> element

```
<template id="commentTemplate">
  <div>
    <img src="">
    <div class="comment-text"></div>
  </div>
</template>
<script>
function addComment(imageUrl, text) {
  var t = document.querySelector("#commentTemplate");
  var comment = t.content.cloneNode(true);

  // Populate content.
  comment.querySelector('img').src = imageUrl;
  comment.querySelector('.comment-text').textContent = text;
  document.body.appendChild(comment);
}
</script>
```

In this example, I've created a simple <template> element to hold some DOM that represents a comment block on a blog. The block contains a source-less image and an empty div for the text. In the next script block, I have an addComment function that takes an image URL and some text. The function then selects my template block, clones it into a new `HTMLElement` object, sets the image and text values, and then appends the DOM fragment to the body of the document. At that final step, the browser parses and renders the template-based content.

As I said, it should seem familiar, because it is. Thankfully, having first-class template support in the browser means we can put all of those templating libraries to rest and use speedy, built-in functionality.

Shadow DOM

The next Web Components spec is Shadow DOM (*http://bit.ly/dom-shadow*), a feature that allows developers to encapsulate DOM subtrees and hide widget implementation details. It sounds a bit cryptic, I know, so let's take a look at Shadow DOM in the context of an HTML element already using this capability: the HTML `<video>` tag.

Take a look at Figure 6-3. What do you see? A rectangle with a video canvas and several controls, right? Right, but have you ever wondered how the browsers actually implement tags like `<video>` and `<audio>`?

Figure 6-3. An HTML `<video>` element in action

With the Chrome Developer Tools, you can find out. All you need to do is open your Chrome DevTools and click the gear icon in the lower-right corner. Then, look for the "Show Shadow DOM" option and make sure that it's checked. Then, you can navigate to any page with a `<video>` tag, right-click it, and select "Inspect Element."

What you'll see looks like Figure 6-4. Inside the innocent-looking `<video>` tag lies `<divs>`, `<inputs>`, buttons, and more. Browser vendors like Google actually use standard HTML tags and inputs—though the specific tags are up to the vendor—to create complex visual elements like `<video>`. Shadow DOM is, simply put, the technology that allows Chrome and other browsers to hide those implementation details behind a single tag that developers can rely on.

Figure 6-4. Shadow DOM in action

By making Shadow DOM developer-accessible and supported in the browsers, we can do the same. We can build our own complex widgets and features that are easy for developers to use, but that also hide their implementation details and can even prevent unauthorized access to subelements and widget styles.

Custom Elements

The next Web Components technology is Custom Elements (*http://bit.ly/custom-ele*). Custom Elements provide a formal way for developers to create their own valid HTML tags and define the API for those elements. You can also extend the semantics and behavior of existing elements, as shown in Example 6-8.

Example 6-8. Defining a custom element that extends the `<button>` element

```
<!-- Define the element -->
<element extends="button" name="fancy-button">
  <style>
    @host {
```

```
      font-size: 20em; /* make it huge */
      color: salmon; /* make it BOLD! */
    }
  </style>
  <content></content>
</element>

<!-- Put it to use -->
<button is="fancy-button">Do something fancy</button>
```

Here, I'm using the new `<element>` element to define a Custom Element that extends `<button>` with a larger font size and a default color. Then, when I want to put my Custom Element to use, I'll create a `<button>` element on the page—if this was a completely new element, I'd use my custom tag—and use the `is` attribute to tell the parser that this is my Custom Element. With Custom Elements, it's that easy to add your own semantics and behavior to HTML.

HTML Imports

The final piece of the Web Components umbrella is HTML Imports (*http://bit.ly/html-imports*). This is the most straightforward of the Web Components specs. Simply put, Imports provide a mechanism for importing Templates and Custom Elements into a site or app. For instance, let's say that I define my fancy-button element from Example 6-8 in a separate file called *fancy-button.html*. HTML Imports provide the mechanism for, well, importing this element into my app, as shown in Example 6-9.

Example 6-9. Using imports with custom elements

```
<!DOCTYPE html>
<html>
  <head>
    <link rel="import" href="fancy-button.html">
  </head>
  <body>
    <button is="fancy-button"></button>
     <!-- Element definition is in fancy-button.html -->
  </body>
</html>
```

Imports are enabled via a new `rel` value of `import` on the HTML `link` element. When this value is encountered, the browser will load the linked element and make it available to my app. HTML Imports are a simple concept, but an important one because they enable me to manage Custom Elements and Templates in separate files.

Web Components hold a lot of promise for the future, but because most of the ideas are still very cutting edge, they don't enjoy wide browser support. Templates and Shadow DOM are supported in Chrome and Firefox, but, at the time of writing, there's not a single browser that supports all four of the specs. If we want to start building and using

Custom Elements today, we need a prollyfill! At present, there are two ways to start working with Custom Elements: one approach that's available via a popular open source library, and another that requires adopting a bleeding-edge prollyfill provided by members of the Google Chrome team.

Creating Custom Elements with AngularJS

If the idea of creating your own semantics in HTML is appealing, but you're not as concerned with formally prollyfilling Web Components, you might want to take a look at AngularJS. If you're familiar with AngularJS, you're no doubt aware of the directives feature of the library, which allows you to link imperative functionality to declarative semantics via HTML elements and attributes. For instance, let's say that I want to create a <calendar> element that will, via an AngularJS directive, create a Kendo UI Calendar widget. The Angular code I need to enable this can be seen in Example 6-10.

Example 6-10. Creating custom elements via AngularJS directives

```
<div ng-app="myApp">
  <calendar></calendar>
</div>
<script>
angular.module('myApp', []).directive('calendar', function() {
  return {
    restrict: 'F',
    link: function(scope, element, attrs) {
      $(element).kendoCalendar();
    }
  }
});
</script>
```

Notice that AngularJS enables me to go all out and use my directive via a <calendar> element on my page. It's a nice trick, for sure, but it's not valid HTML. What's more, AngularJS's approach wasn't built with Web Components in mind, so we couldn't classify it as a prollyfill. If we're interested in something that's built with Web Components in mind, we need to look no further than the Polymer project.

Creating Custom Elements with Polymer

Polymer (*http://polymer-project.org*) is a Google-sponsored project designed to speed up the adoption of cutting-edge web platform technologies by providing a series of robust prollyfills that work across evergreen browsers. The Polymer project actually provides a number of prollyfills, but the core of the offering is support for Shadow DOM, Templates, Custom Elements, and HTML Imports.

In our discussion on Web Components, I shared some code snippets meant to communicate the "perfect world" approach for building components, as defined by the current draft of each spec. Polymer enables us to create Web Components using much of the same syntax, with only a few small differences.

At the time of writing, the Polymer authors are careful to note that the library is in an Alpha state. You'll want to keep this in mind when using, or even installing, the library.

Let's say, for instance, and in keeping with our previous AngularJS example, that I want to create a custom <calendar> element that provides a declarative way of working with a Kendo UI Calendar widget. To create my custom element with Polymer, I'll create a new file called *x-calendar.html* and populate it with my custom element definition, as illustrated in Example 6-11:

Example 6-11. Creating a <calendar> custom element with Polymer

```
<script src="jquery-1.10.2.min.js"></script>
<!-- Kendo UI Scripts -->
<script src="kendo.web.min.js"></script>

<polymer-element name="x-calendar" attributes="selected">
  <link rel="stylesheet" href="kendo.common.min.css">
  <link rel="stylesheet" href="kendo.default.min.css">

  <!-- Element Here -->
  <template>
    <div id="calendar"></div>
  </template>
  <script>
  Polymer('x-calendar', {
    selected: new Date(),
    created: function() {
      $(this.$.calendar).kendoCalendar({
        value: this.selected
      });
    }
  });
  </script>
</polymer-element>
```

While the syntax for my element is similar to the Custom Elements spec, there are a few key differences. First, instead of using the proposed <element> element, I use <polymer-element>. Inside my <polymer-element> declaration, I give my element a name that, according to the Custom Elements spec, must always contain a dash. I use the at tributes attribute to specify a list of properties that I want to publish on my element. Published attributes become part of the public API for my element, which allows them to be set declaratively via HTML or JavaScript.

The second Polymer-specific aspect to this element is the call to the Polymer method. This method formally registers my custom element so that it can be used in my app while also setting the default values for properties (`selected`) and subscribing to element life-cycle events. In this example, I'm subscribing to the `created` event, which fires when a new instance of my custom element is used in an app. When my event callback fires, I create a new Kendo UI Calendar from the current element and set its current date to either the default date or the user-specified date.

The rest of the process of working with custom elements in Polymer is pretty straightforward, as illustrated in Example 6-12. In this sample, the key difference is in the `<head>`, where I include the minified Polymer source. When included, Polymer does everything required to work with my custom element import, process the element, and then render the element when called upon. The end result of the snippet in Example 6-12 is a full Kendo UI Calendar with a selected date of October 5, 2013. To the component-consuming developer, it's a totally declarative approach that works great across browsers, thanks to Polymer.

Example 6-12. Using Polymer elements

```
<!DOCTYPE html>
  <html lang="en">
  <head>
    <title>Polymer Calendar</title>
        <script src="lib/js/polymer.min.js"></script>

    <!-- Import Calendar -->
    <link rel="import" href="components/x-calendar.html">
  </head>
  <body>
    <div class="container">
      <div class="jumbotron">
        <!-- Calendar here -->
        <h1>What day is it?</h1>
        <x-calendar selected="2013/10/05"></x-calendar>
      </div>
    </div>
  </body>
</html>
```

Strategies for Polyfilling Experimental APIs

Over the course of this chapter, we've discussed a handful of great prollyfilling libraries that allow us to experiment with new and cutting-edge ideas in CSS, HTML, and Java-Script. In the next and final chapter of this book, we're going to try our hand at constructing our own prollyfill. But before we do, let's look briefly at a few things to keep in mind when building prollyfills for untested or experimental APIs.

Expect the API to Change

One of the key differences between classical polyfills and future-leaning prollyfills is in the API. As we discussed in early chapters, a key to building a robust, responsible polyfill is in respecting the specified API for the feature you're looking to fill. Prollyfills, however, are built to work with bleeding-edge features. Sometimes there is no specified API because you're the first person to explore this idea. In other cases, the specification is so new and unstable that you can expect the API to change before things settle down. In either case, you're building your prollyfill against something of a moving target, so it's important to think about how to design with a flexible API in mind. There are no quick answers here other than to make sure that the public API for your prollyfill is flexible from the outset, easy to change, and, when it does change, that you can quickly change your online samples, docs, and demos.

Don't Be Afraid to Try Something New

Prollyfilling is all about experimentation. It's about taking cutting-edge ideas and building a library that allows you and other developers to put those ideas to the test. It's about refining those ideas, suggesting changes, and even taking those ideas in a totally new direction. If you're building a prollyfill, you're likely not doing so with the goal of getting some new web platform feature into your production apps tomorrow. Instead, you've probably undertaken a prollyfill because you want to play a role in moving the Web forward. In that spirit, you should feel free to think and innovate well outside the box as you work on your library. If, when building a prollyfill for a new spec or proposal, you encounter something you don't like in the spec, or a new feature you want to see added, build your argument right into the library. Code speaks louder than words on the Web, and if you can communicate a counter proposal, changes, or a new idea in the context of a working sample that also highlights some aspects of a specified feature, you make your argument that much more powerful.

Now that we've explored the ins and outs of prollyfilling, and some high-level strategies for building our own prollyfills, let's turn our attention to building a prollyfill of our own. In the next chapter, we'll take a brand new web platform feature and craft a simple prollyfill for it.

CHAPTER 7

Building Your First Prollyfill

In Chapters 3 through 5, I walked you through the exercise of building a polyfill for the HTML5 Forms spec. Over the course of those three chapters, we talked about how to make a plan for building a polyfill, how to go about initial development, how to configure your library for automated and cross-browser testing, and finally, how to build your polyfill for performance.

In Chapter 6, I introduced the concept of the prollyfill and walked through several examples of popular prollyfilling libraries. In this chapter, we're going to build on that knowledge, along with what we learned earlier in the book, and build our own prollyfill to test out an experimental web platform feature. Along the way, you'll learn the ways that building polyfills and prollyfills are similar, and the ways they differ.

Prollyfills vs. Polyfills: What's the Difference?

Prollyfills, as we discussed in Chapter 6, are quite similar to polyfills in many ways, the biggest difference being that they often target proposals or specifications with in-flux APIs. Sometimes they even target untested or unspecified ideas altogether. In both cases, much of the ideas that surround the prollyfill, including the API, are expected to change greatly as the idea is debated, tested, and possibly accepted for standardization.

In addition, the purpose of building a prollyfill differs from that of a polyfill. Polyfills are typically built to allow developers to rely on new features and APIs across all browsers. They are meant, for the most part, to be used in production apps by everyday developers. Prollyfills are different. In many ways, these libraries are experiments. They are built to test out unproven concepts, or ideas for standardization that need developer feedback or real-world application. Prollyfills are, for the most part, meant to be used in development and test settings, and not in production apps.

That key difference between prollyfills and polyfills—their purpose for being—tells us a great deal about how these libraries can and should be built by developers. As you'll see in this chapter, much of the construction process remains the same. You'll still want to set up unit tests and cross-browser tests and plan out the scope of your library, but you'll also need to build flexibility into the API of the library, which you should expect to change. You'll want to pay attention to performance, of course, but it's less critical with a prollyfill since these libraries are meant to test ideas. Often prollyfills will lead you to create implementations that can't be optimized for speed, but as you'll see in this chapter, that's perfectly OK.

The Resource Priorities Prollyfill

For the rest of this chapter, we're going to go through a brief exercise and build our own prollyfill for a brand-new W3C proposal. The name of the specification we'll be targeting is Resource Priorities (*http://bit.ly/reso-prior*). Resource priorities are meant to provide developers with new HTML attributes and a CSS property that can be used to specify the download priority of a resource like an image, script, or media element. The two attributes and property are as follows:

lazyload *(http://bit.ly/rp-lazy)*
> A Boolean HTML attribute that tells the browser to delay loading resources specified by the element in question until all elements that do not have this attribute have started downloading.

postpone *(http://bit.ly/rp-postp)*
> A Boolean HTML attribute that tells the browser to delay loading resources specified by the element in question until the element or its container are visible in the viewport.

resource-priorities *(http://bit.ly/priorities-att)*
> A CSS property that can be used to set the download priority (lazyload or post pone) of a resource associated with an element or another CSS property.

You're probably wondering what the point of this spec is, especially in light of HTML5's defer and async attributes. For starters, defer and async are available only to <script> elements, whereas lazyload and postpone are available to all HTML elements that can download resources, including script, link, img, audio, video, iframe, and more.

More important, though, resource priorities provide developers with a way to programmatically give the browser hints as to the importance of external resources. At the present, download priority for the browser is based solely on document order—scripts, stylesheets, and images are loaded in the order that they appear. But document order, especially for visual resources, is often more a function of document location and not resource importance. As a result, it's difficult for developers to control the real and perceived performance of their pages without script-based hacks.

Let's take a look at an example. The page in Example 7-1 contains several resources: two stylesheets, a video, several images, and a few scripts. The way this document is structured, all media will be downloaded in document order, and our script at app.js, which presumably is important to the function of the page, won't start executing until those downloads have at least initiated. What's more, if our app.js script is relying on a document.load event or jQuery's load event, our application script won't load until those resources have been loaded.

Example 7-1. An example HTML page, sample.html, with document-order prioritized resources

```
<!DOCTYPE html>
<html>
  <head>
    <link rel="stylesheet" type="text/css" src="styles.css" />
    <link rel="stylesheet" type="text/css" src="animations.css" />
  </head>
  <body>
    <img id="siteLogo" src="/images/site.png"/>
    <img id="Header" src="/images/Header.png"/>
    <ul class="gallery">
      <li>
        <img id="img1" src=".../images/img1.png" />
      </li>
      <li>
        <img id="img3" src=".../images/img2.png" />
      </li>
      <li>
        <img id="img3" src=".../images/img3.png" />
      </li>
    </ul>
    <video class="promo">
      <source src="/videos/promo.mp4">
      <source src="/videos/promo.ogv">
      <source src="/videos/promo.webm">
    </video>
    <script src="app.js" ></script>
    <script src="GoogleAnalytics.js"></script>
  </body>
</html>
```

The lazyload and postpone properties provide us an alternative that allows us to preserve our page structure, while also providing programmatic hints as to the importance of page resources. Elements with lazyload and postpone will be loaded either when all other resources have been loaded or when the viewport enters the bounding box of the element in question, respectively. Elements without either of these properties, on the other hand, will continue to load in document order, as before. Example 7-2 shows these features in action.

Example 7-2. An example HTML page, sample.html, with prioritized resources

```html
<!DOCTYPE html>
<html>
  <head>
    <link rel="stylesheet" type="text/css" src="styles.css" />
    <link rel="stylesheet" type="text/css" src="animations.css" lazyload />
    <style>
      video.promo source {
        resource-priorities: postpone;
      }
    </style>
  </head>
  <body>
    <img id="siteLogo" src="/images/site.png"/>
    <img id="Header" src="/images/Header.png"/>
    <ul class="gallery">
      <li>
        <img id="img1" src=".../images/img1.png" lazyload />
      </li>
      <li>
        <img id="img3" src=".../images/img2.png" postpone />
      </li>
      <li>
        <img id="img3" src=".../images/img3.png" postpone />
      </li>
    </ul>
    <video class="promo">
      <source src="/videos/promo.mp4">
      <source src="/videos/promo.ogv">
      <source src="/videos/promo.webm">
    </video>
        <script src="app.js" ></script>
    <script src="GoogleAnalytics.js" lazyload></script>
  </body>
</html>
```

In this sample, which will also serve as our base demo page for the prollyfill, you can see both attributes and the property in action. First, in the `<style>` tag, we have a single CSS selector for the source values of any `<video>` tags containing the class `promo`. Inside the selector is our `resource-priorities` property, which tells the browser to set the `postpone` value on the video source elements, which will ensure that the video on my page doesn't begin loading until the user scrolls to that location on the screen.

Throughout the rest of the sample, I've applied the `lazyload` attribute to those resources that I want to have downloaded as soon as core page resources are loaded, and the `postpone` attribute to those resources that need to be loaded only when in the user's visible viewport. The end result is a page with clear instructions to the browser as to the loading priority of all resources in the document.

Resource priorities are a great idea, but since they are so new, there aren't any native browser implementations. So we'll build our own prollyfill, which will allow us and other developers to put this spec through its paces and offer feedback to spec authors and the W3C. Let's get started building that prollyfill, which I've decided to call *slacker.js* in what was probably a misguided attempt to be clever.

Specifying the API and Deciding What to Build

Before beginning construction of our prollyfill, it's important to take a moment and consider the purpose and goals of the project, what you will and won't take on, as well as the API of the library. As I did in Chapter 2 with the HTML5 Forms polyfill, the first thing I did with `slacker.js` (*http://bit.ly/slacker-js*) was to define the purpose and goals of the project, as described here:

Purpose and Goals

The purpose of this project is to serve as a complete prollyfill for the draft Resource Priorities spec, including support for new HTML attributes (`lazyload` and `postpone`), a new CSS property (`resource-priorities`), and a DOM event (`lazyloaded`). This project includes built-in feature detection and, by default, will polyfill only those forms features not present in the user's browser.

As a prollyfill, this library's primary purpose is to serve as a proof-of-concept and test bed for conversations around the Resource Priorities specification, and *not* to serve as a cross-browser polyfill ready for production use.

This library will function as both a drop-in and opt-in prollyfill, depending on the features being used. For the `lazyload` and `postpone` properties, this library will manage resources when these attributes are included in a document and the `data-href` or `data-src` attribute is used. When using the `resource-priorities` CSS property, `link` and `style` elements should be decorated with an attribute (`data-slacker-interpret`) that will indicate use of this property to the prollyfill.

Goals

- Provide a complete Resource Priorities solution that allows developers to experiment with new attributes, CSS properties, and DOM events, as defined in the spec.

- Provide a test bed for specified and experimental features. As a prollyfill, the API surface of this library is not limited to those features already contained in the spec. Where it makes sense to propose new or changed features, this library can be used as a POC for those proposed changes.

- Adapt quickly to specification changes, including those to the spec's API. We expect this spec to change, and this library should be built in such a way that API changes are easy to absorb.

- This library is intended to serve as a proof-of-concept for a cutting-edge web platform feature, and as such is not meant for production use.

- As a proof-of-concept, this library will not be performance-tuned.

- This library may diverge from the Resource Priorities spec (*http://bit.ly/reso-prior*) in order to add convenience features, nonstandard behaviors, or experimental APIs for consideration by spec authors.

As you can see, this section has a lot of similarities to and differences from our Forms polyfill. Like the Forms Library, this section contains a summary of the purpose of the project, as well as a few bullets covering the goals and non-goals of the project. The differences are clear in the content, however. Our prollyfill is an experiment intended to drive discussion, and you can see that reflected in the preceding text.

Once I've clearly defined the purpose and goals of my library, I'll turn my attention next to its API. For this, I like to sit down with the spec and draft a features matrix so that I can outline the major features my library should provide, as well as any feature-specific caveats, opt-in features, or quirks that the library should account for. Table 7-1 illustrates my initial features matrix for `slacker.js`.

Table 7-1. Features matrix for `slacker.js`

Feature	Opt-in	Workflow and Exceptions	Supported Elements
Support for `lazy load` attribute	Yes (data-src/data-href)	Remove `src` of elements with `lazyload` and place in an array. When `document.load` is fired, reset the `src` for each element. For `script`, if `defer` is used with `lazyload`, it has no effect. For `script`, if `async` is set to `false`, `lazyload` has no effect; for `svg reImage`, if `externalResourcesRe quired` is set to `true`, `lazyload` has no effect.	`img`, `audio`, `video`, `script`, `link`, `embed`, `iframe`, `object`, `svg fe Image`, `svg use`, `svg script`, `svg tref`
Support for `post pone` attribute	Yes (data-src/data-href)	Remove `src` of elements with `postpone` and place in an array. On scroll or when an element with the `dis play:none` property becomes visible, determine if any elements are within the bounding box of the page and if so, reset the `src` for each visible element. For `au dio`, `postpone` works only if the `controls` attribute has been set; for `svg reImage`, if `exter nalResourcesRequired` is set to `true`, `post pone` has no effect.	`img`, `audio`, `video`, `script`, `link`, `embed`, `iframe`, `object`, `svg re Image`, `svg use`, `svg script`, `svg tref`

Feature	Opt-In	Workflow and Exceptions	Supported Elements
Support for resource-priorities CSS property	Yes (data-slacker-interpret)	Parse all `link` and `style` elements that use the `data-slacker-interpret` attribute and find all instances of the `resource-priorities` property. Remove `src` values for related elements, and any CSS properties that specify a source (like `background-image`). No exceptions.	`img`, `audio`, `video`, `script`, `link`, `embed`, `iframe`, `object`, `svg re Image`, `svg use`, `svg script`, `svg tref`, `background-image`, `border-image-source`, `content`, `cursor`, `list-style-image`, `@font-face src`
Support for `lazy loaded` event	No	Once the `src` has been reset for resources with the `lazyload` attribute, fire the `lazyloaded` event. If no such elements exist, fire immediately after `document.load`. No exceptions.	N/A

Even though there are really only four major features to the Resource Priorities spec, there's quite a lot going on for what seems like a relatively straightforward prollyfill. In addition to needing to support new attributes, a CSS property, and a DOM event, we have to consider how to support these new features across a dozen HTML elements and a handful of resource-loading CSS properties. We also have to take into account the interaction between `lazyload`/`postpone` and `defer` and `async` when used on script elements. Since there's a lot to consider when building my prollyfill, I'm going to create a road map for major features, just as I did for my HTML5 Forms polyfill. The road map for `slacker.js` can be seen here:

- v0.1—support for the `lazyload` attribute and `lazyloaded` event
- v0.2—support for the `postpone` attribute
- v0.5—support for the `resource-priorities` CSS property
- v1.0—full spec support (v0.5 + bug-fixes and enhancements)

With a clearly defined set of goals, features, and a road map for my library, I'm now ready to get started. In the next section, we'll set up the initial project for `slacker.js` and start building out our polyfill.

Setting Up Your Prollyfill Project

In Chapter 3, I provided some tips on how to set up the initial project structure for your polyfill, including essential documentation files (*README, LICENSE, CHANGELOG, CONTRIBUTING*) and essential directories for your source, third party dependencies, tests, and distribution files. In Chapter 4, we expanded on this list with a discussion on configuring project builds with Grunt and setting up unit and cross-browser testing via Jasmine, Karma, and Travis. For a prollyfill, much of this process remains the same, so

I won't repeat it here. Instead, I encourage you to check out Chapters 3 and 4 if you haven't already to get an overview of how I've chosen to configure both my HTML5 Forms polyfill and my Resource Priorities prollyfill.

Adding Prollyfill Features

For slacker.js, I'm going to use Jasmine (*http://bit.ly/jas-lib*) for my unit tests, just as I did for the HTML5 Forms polyfill earlier in the book. Once I've configured Jasmine, including the Grunt- and Karma-dependent steps outlined in Chapter 4, I'm ready to add my first test.

The First Test: Feature Detection

In the road map for my prollyfill, which I shared previously, I decided to first focus on supporting the lazyload attribute. Along those lines, my first test makes sure that my prollyfill is performing feature detection for the lazyload attribute. I know, of course, that no browser currently supports this attribute, but I don't know how long that will be the case, or how long my library will stick around, so the responsible thing to do is to always perform feature detection, if possible, even when building prollyfills. Example 7-3 contains the source for my first test.

If you're using Chrome, some tests will fail because of cross-domain restrictions. To work around this, you'll want to either run your tests using a local web server, or run Chrome with the --allow-file-access-from-files terminal command.

For OS X, run open -a /Applications/Google\ Chrome.app --args --allow-file-access-from-files.

And for Windows, run C:\Users\[UserName]\AppData\Local\Google\Chrome[SxS] \Application\chrome.exe --allow-file-access-from-files.

Example 7-3. First test in fixtures.js for the slacker.js *prollyfill*

```
var path = 'javascripts/fixtures/';

describe('lazyload attribute tests', function() {
  it('should test for the lazyload attribute before acting', function() {
    var s = document.createElement('script');
    var lazyloadSupported = 'lazyload' in s;
    var slackerFrame = document.querySelector('iframe#slackerFrame'),
      loaded = false;

    slackerFrame.src = path + 'lazyload.html';
    slackerFrame.addEventListener('load', function() {
      loaded = true;
    });

    waitsFor(function() {
```

```
      return loaded;
    }, 'iframe load event never fired', 2000);

    runs(function() {
      expect(lazyloadSupported)
        .toEqual(slackerFrame.contentWindow.slacker.features.lazyload);

      slackerFrame.src = '';
    });
  });
});
```

There's quite a lot going on here, so let's unpack this sample. The first thing you'll notice is that I'm getting a reference to an iframe in my main document. This is key. Because my prollyfill is meant to operate on entire documents, I feel that I should simulate these conditions as much as possible in my tests. In order to do that, I load an external HTML file, the source of which is shown in Example 7-4, and inject it as the source of my iframe, which causes my prollyfill to run. Once I've loaded the iframe and set its new source, I need to wait for the page to fully load before running my tests, so I add an event listener for the frame and use the Jasmine `waitsFor` and `runs` methods to make sure that the tests don't run until I'm good and ready.

Example 7-4. The lazyload.html source

```
<!DOCTYPE html>
<html>
<head>
  <link rel="stylesheet" type="text/css" href="styles.css" />
  <link rel="stylesheet" type="text/css" data-href="animations.css" lazyload />
</head>
<body>
  <img data-src="foo.png" lazyload/>

  <script src="../../../../src/slacker.features.js"></script>
  <script src="../../../../src/slacker.js"></script>
</body>
</html>
```

When I first run this test, it will fail, of course. In order to make it pass, I'll add a test for the `lazyload` attribute to my source in a new file called *slacker.features.js*, as shown in Example 7-5.

Example 7-5. lazyload feature test in slacker.js

```
(function() {
  window.slacker = window.slacker || {};

  var resourcePrioritiesFeatures = {
    lazyload: (function () {
      var s = document.createElement('script');
      return 'lazyload' in s;
```

```
    })()
  };

  window.slacker.features = resourcePrioritiesFeatures;
}());
```

This module, which will serve as the core module for all feature tests in my prollyfill,
starts with an IIFE before setting the global `window.slacker` namespace that I'll be using
for the library. Next, I create an object literal to hold my feature tests, and add a test for
the `lazyload`. As discussed in Chapter 3, I can test for official support for new HTML
attributes by creating an in-memory element and checking to see whether the attribute
exists. Once I've added my features module and the `lazyload` test, my first test should
pass.

The Second Test: Initial lazyload Functionality

Now that I have my feature testing in place, I can shift to the `lazyload` attribute itself.
The next test, as illustrated in Example 7-6, will make sure that my prollyfill detects the
presence of this attribute and removes whatever value is specified in the `data-href`
attribute of my `<link>` element.

Example 7-6. Testing data-href attribute removal in fixtures.js

```
it('should detect the lazyload attribute and remove data-href',
function() {
  var slackerFrame = document.querySelector('iframe#slackerFrame'),
    loaded = false;

  slackerFrame.src = path + '/lazyload.html';
  slackerFrame.addEventListener('load', function() {
    loaded = true;
  });

  waitsFor(function() {
    return loaded;
  }, 'iframe load event never fired', 2000);

  runs(function() {
    var stylesheet = slackerFrame.contentDocument.querySelectorAll('link[lazyload]');

    expect(stylesheet.length).not.toBe(0);
    expect(stylesheet[0].getAttribute('data-href')).toEqual('');

    slackerFrame.src = '';
  });
});
```

This test is similar to our first in that it does some async work to prepare an iframe—
and we'll clean up this duplication in a bit—before running the actual test. The test pulls

---

the `<link>` element from the DOM and checks to see that its `data-href` attribute is `null`. As with our first test, this test will fail on first run because I haven't added any functionality yet. Let's do that, first by creating a *slacker.js* source file in the *src/* directory for my project, and then by adding the `src` removal functionality, as illustrated in Example 7-7.

Example 7-7. Creating the `lazyload` src removal feature in slacker.js

```
(function() {
  window.slacker = window.slacker || {};

  var i, len,
    lazyLoaded = [];

  //Test for the presence of the lazyload attribute.
  //If it's not supported, let's get to work.
  if (!window.slacker.features.lazyload){
    var elements = document.querySelectorAll('[lazyload]');

    for (i = 0, len = elements.length; i < len; i++) {
      var el = elements[i];
      if (el.nodeName === 'LINK') {
        lazyLoaded.push(el.getAttribute('data-href'));
        el.setAttribute('data-href','');
      }
    }
  }

}());
```

At this point, our prollyfill is pretty simple, but it's enough to make our second test pass. I'm simply looking for every element with the `lazyloaded` attribute and then looping over each. If the `nodeName` of the current element is `LINK`, I remove that element's `data-href` attribute and place it into an array. If I run my tests again, they should now pass.

The First Refactor: Cleaning Up the Tests

At this point, our prollyfill is nowhere near functional, but we're off to the right start. A logical next step would be to round out basic `lazyload` support by setting my `link` element's `href` after the page load. We'll get to that, of course, but first I need to clean up some duplication of code in my tests in order to simplify things.

If you take a look at Example 7-3 and Example 7-6, you'll notice a lot of boilerplate test code that I have to duplicate each time through. I'd like to clean this up to make my subsequent tests cleaner, so I'll create a local function in my *fixtures.js* file to manage all of the frame loading. The source of this helper method can be found in Example 7-8.

Example 7-8. The test runner helper method in fixtures.js

```
function loadFrame(test) {
  var slackerFrame = document.querySelector('iframe#slackerFrame'),
    loaded = false;

  slackerFrame.src = path + 'lazyload.html';
  slackerFrame.addEventListener('load', function() {
    loaded = true;
  });

  waitsFor(function() {
    return loaded;
  }, 'iframe load event never fired', 2000);

  runs(function() {
    if (test && typeof test === 'function') {
      test(slackerFrame);
    }

    slackerFrame.src = '';
  });
}
```

With this method, I'm able to abstract away much of the iframe logic and keep my test methods clean so that they have to pass in only the spec-specific setup and expect statements. As an example, my refactored version of Example 7-3 can be seen in Example 7-9. It's much cleaner and will make adding subsequent tests much simpler.

Example 7-9. A refactored iframe test in fixtures.js

```
it('should test for the lazyload attribute before acting', function() {
  var s = document.createElement('script');
  var lazyloadSupported = 'lazyload' in s;

  loadFrame(function(frame) {
    expect(lazyloadSupported)
      .toEqual(frame.contentWindow.slacker.features.lazyload);
  });
});
```

The Third Test: Modifying the Public API

So far, we've been building our prollyfill to the Resource Priorities spec, and things look pretty good. However, as a prollyfill developer, you might encounter situations where you have an idea for a feature of your library that might actually make sense as a part of the official spec. In this section, we'll explore the addition of one such feature to slacker.js.

As I worked on the initial functionality for slacker.js, I found myself wishing that the collection of deprioritized elements—as in, those decorated with the lazyload or postpone attributes—were available in some form of collection that I could inspect from my tests. I also thought that a collection like this would be useful to app developers, so since this is a prollyfill for a draft specification, what better way to test out this idea than to add the feature to my prollyfill and try it out?

To add this functionality, I'll start with a simple test, as illustrated in Example 7-10. Here, I'm specifying that I expect for my slacker object to hold an array called lazyLoaded and that this array should have a length of 2, which corresponds to the two elements (one <link> and one <img>) in my *lazyload.html* test file.

Example 7-10. Testing for brand-new functionality in fixtures.js

```
it('should hold the resource source in the lazyLoaded array', function() {
  loadFrame(function(frame) {
    var win = frame.contentWindow;
    expect(win.slacker.lazyLoaded.length).toEqual(2);
  });
});
```

Once I've added this test and run my tests in the browser to verify failure, I'll head back over to slacker.js to add the following line just after the for loop:

```
window.slacker.lazyLoaded = lazyLoaded;
```

With this line, my tests and apps can now obtain access to an array of lazyloaded elements. Is this a good idea? Maybe or maybe not. All that matters in this case is that, as a prollyfill developer, I should feel free to experiment and play with ideas like this, and even pitch them to the spec authors for inclusion. If they say yes, I've contributed to a future web platform standard! And if not, no harm, no foul. I can simply remove the API from my prollyfill and move on, confident that I've still contributed to the standardization process by encouraging conversation.

Of course, if this new API were to be added to the spec, it would no doubt live as an object on window and would probably have a different name. I'm adding it to my slacker namespace to be clear about the API for my prollyfill. If and when I propose this new addition, I can use the API of my library as a reference, while suggesting additions or changes to the spec.

The Fourth Test: Supporting Additional Element Types

My test in Example 7-10 will still fail at this point, and if you look at the source in Example 7-7, it's easy to see why. My test file contains two lazyload elements, an image, and a stylesheet, but my prollyfill supports only the <link> element, so I'll need to modify the library to support the <img> element as well. Example 7-11 contains the new source of my for loop.

Example 7-11. Supporting a second element type in `slacker.js`

```
for (i = 0, len = elements.length; i < len; i++) {
  var el = elements[i];
  if (el.nodeName === 'LINK') {
    lazyLoaded.push(el.getAttribute('data-href'));
    el.setAttribute('data-href','');
  } else if (el.nodeName === 'IMG') {
    lazyLoaded.push(el.getAttribute('data-src'));
    el.setAttribute('data-src','');
  }
}
```

Once I've added this code, the test in Example 7-10 will pass, meaning that I have starter support for two element types and a public object that holds my `lazyLoaded` URLs. This is great, but since there's some code duplication—and I hate duplication—it's time for another refactor.

The Second Refactor: Completing Element Type Support

With only two elements to support, my `if` statement isn't too unwieldy. That said, according to the Resource Priorities spec, I need to support 13 element types. What's more, I still have to add support for `postpone`, which also supports 13 elements. I really don't want to keep adding `if` statements, so it's time for another refactor.

Since the only real difference between the elements I need to support is the source attribute they use (`href` or `src`), I can do a lot to abstract away the clearing of attributes into a local helper method, while placing each element I want to support into a local object. The new source for `slacker.js` once I've made this change can be found in Example 7-12.

Example 7-12. Refactoring to add multiple element support in `slacker.js`

```
(function() {
  window.slacker = window.slacker || {};

  var i, len,
    lazyLoaded = [];

  function clearSourceAttribute(el, attr) {
    lazyLoaded.push(el.getAttribute(attr));
    el.setAttribute(attr,'');
  }

  var elementReplacements = {
    LINK: function(el) {
      clearSourceAttribute(el, 'data-href');
    },
    IMG: function(el) {
      clearSourceAttribute(el, 'data-src');
```

```
    }
  };

  //Test for the presence of the lazyload attribute.
  //If it's not supported, let's get to work.
  if (!window.slacker.features.lazyload){
    var elements = document.querySelectorAll('[lazyload]');

    for (i = 0, len = elements.length; i < len; i++) {
      var el = elements[i];

      if (el.nodeName in elementReplacements) {
        elementReplacements[el.nodeName](el);
      }
    }
    //Make the array of lazyLoaded elements publicly available
    //for debugging.
    window.slacker.lazyLoaded = lazyLoaded;
  }

}());
```

By moving most of the attribute support and element-specific logic into module-level functions, I get a much cleaner for loop. It's also much easier to add support for the rest of the elements in the spec. Let's add another one of those now, first via a test, as shown in Example 7-13.

Example 7-13. Testing for <script> element support in fixtures.js

```
it('should support the script element', function() {
  loadFrame(function(frame) {
    var stylesheet = frame.contentDocument.querySelectorAll('script[lazyload]');

    expect(stylesheet.length).not.toBe(0);
    expect(stylesheet[0].getAttribute('data-src')).toEqual('');
  });
});
```

Similar to my initial test for the link attribute, I'm making sure that my <script> element is in the page, and that my prollyfill removes its data-src attribute. After verifying that it fails, I can add support to the slacker.js source by adding a new function for the <script> element, as shown in Example 7-14. Once I've added this function, I can rerun my tests and confirm that they pass.

Example 7-14. Adding support for the <script> element in slacker.js

```
var elementReplacements = {
  LINK: function(el) {
    clearSourceAttribute(el, 'data-href');
  },
  IMG: function(el) {
```

```
      clearSourceAttribute(el, 'data-src');
    },
    SCRIPT: function(el) {
      clearSourceAttribute(el, 'data-src');
    }
};
```

The Fifth Test: Completing Initial Support

Now that I have some initial functionality to remove resource source attributes, and I
have a clean way to add support for all element types, it's time to complete initial support
for the lazyloaded attribute by adding functionality to properly set the href attribute
on my link tag after the page load is complete. First, just as we've done every time thus
far, I'll create my failing test, which can be seen in Example 7-15.

Example 7-15. Test for full lazyload attribute support in fixtures.js

```
it('should re-apply the lazyload attribute after the document.load event', function() {
  loadFrame(function(frame) {
    var stylesheet = frame.contentDocument.querySelectorAll('link[lazyload]');

    expect(stylesheet[0].getAttribute('href')).not.toBe(null);
  });
});
```

As per the spec, once the document.load event has fired, I expect my prollyfill to go to
work and set the src and href properties for my elements. If things work properly, this
test will confirm that my test document's link element has been modified accordingly.

To make this test pass, and round out initial support for the lazyloaded attribute, I'll
need to make some pretty extensive changes to my prollyfill source, as shown in
Example 7-16.

Example 7-16. Adding complete support for the lazyloaded attribute in slacker.js

```
(function() {
  window.slacker = window.slacker || {};

  var i, len,
    lazyLoaded = [];

  function clearSourceAttribute(el, attr) {
    lazyLoaded.push({
      el: el,
      source: el.getAttribute('data-' + attr)
    });
    el.setAttribute('data-' + attr,'');
  }

  var elementSource = {
    LINK: 'href',
```

```
      IMG: 'src',
      SCRIPT: 'src'
    };

    //Test for the presence of the lazyload attribute.
    //If it's not supported, let's get to work.
    if (!window.slacker.features.lazyload){
      var elements = document.querySelectorAll('[lazyload]');

      for (i = 0, len = elements.length; i < len; i++) {
        var el = elements[i];

        if (el.nodeName in elementSource) {
          clearSourceAttribute(el, elementSource[el.nodeName]);
        }
      }
      //Make the array of lazyLoaded elements publicly available
      //for debugging.
      window.slacker.lazyLoaded = lazyLoaded;

      //When the page has finished loading, loop through
      //the collection of lazyloaded elements and set their
      //attributes accordingly.
      window.addEventListener('load', function() {
        for (i = 0, len = lazyLoaded.length; i < len; i++) {
          var element = lazyLoaded[i];
          element.el.setAttribute(elementSource[element.el.nodeName], element.source);
        }
      });
    }
}());
```

The key piece of this sample is toward the end, where I've defined a load event listener on the current window. Once that event fires, I know it's time for me to add source properties back on the lazyloaded elements, so I'll loop through my collection of elements and set its src or href property accordingly. If you look closely, you'll also notice that I refactored the clearSourceAttribute function, as well as the elementSource object to support clearing and setting of attributes cleanly. With these changes, all my tests will pass, and all I need to do to support the rest of the specified elements is to add them to the elementSource object. I'll leave that as an exercise for you, though you can also check the public GitHub repo for slacker.js (*http://bit.ly/slacker-js*) if you want to see what the completed prollyfill looks like.

The Final Test: Supporting the lazyloaded Event

Before we close this chapter and our journey into polyfills and prollyfills, there's one more specified feature I want to add. According to the Resource Priorities spec, the browser should fire a lazyloaded DOM event after the download of all the lazyloadmarked documents has been initiated. It should be easy enough to add this, so I'll start again with a failing test (shown in Example 7-17).

Example 7-17. Testing for the `lazyloaded` event in fixtures.js

```
it('should fire the lazyloaded event after src replacement is complete', function() {
  loadFrame(function(frame) {
    var lazyloaded = false;

    frame('lazyloaded', function() {
      lazyloaded = true;
    });

    waitsFor(function() {
      return lazyloaded;
    }, 'iframe lazyloaded event never fired', 2000);

    runs(function() {
      expect(lazyloaded).toBe(true);
    });
  });
});
```

After I load my test document, I'll add a listener for the `lazyloaded` event, and then add the Jasmine `waitsFor` and `runs` functions so that I give the iframe plenty of time to fire the event before I execute the test.

To implement this function, I can add a single line just after the `for` loop in Example 7-16:

```
var evt = new CustomEvent('lazyloaded');
window.dispatchEvent(evt);
```

And that's it! All my tests should pass, and I've now added experimental support for the `lazyload` portion of the Resource Priorities specification.

What's Next?

We breezed through a lot in this chapter for our `slacker.js` prollyfill, but the work is just beginning. From here, I still need to add support for the remaining nine element types, deal with some element-specific edge cases, and then add support for the `post pone` attribute and the `resource-priorities` CSS property. On the infrastructure side, I'll also need to make some changes to account for automated and cross-browser testing. Just like polyfilling, prollyfilling is hard work, and there's still a lot left to do! You can just check out the `slacker.js` GitHub repo (*http://bit.ly/slacker-js*) to see the remaining prollyfill features that I didn't have space to cover here.

Hopefully, over the course of this chapter on building a real-world prollyfill, you got a glimpse into both the similarities and differences between polyfills and prollyfills. The two library types are a lot alike, with the key differences being how you handle the public

API and performance considerations for each. In this section, I'll briefly recap those differences.

Suggesting an API Modification

As we've talked about repeatedly in this book, the public API for a stable feature is set, and should be considered gospel by the polyfill developer. Prollyfills, on the other hand, are in flux, by definition. When building prollyfills, you should respect the API to some extent, while also feeling free to innovate and experiment with new ideas. Adding a `lazyLoaded` collection to `slacker.js` is an example of this.

But no experiment is complete without the reporting of results, so if you like the results of your modifications to an in-flux spec, you should feel free to get in touch with the appropriate working group, mailing list, or directly with the spec authors to get their feedback. As I said in the previous chapter, backing up your ideas with runnable code in a prollyfill is the best way to encourage the right kind of discussion around those ideas.

Building for Performance

As I mentioned earlier in this chapter, when building a prollyfill, your goal is to build something that tests out an experimental API, not to build something meant for cross-browser adoption by developers. As such, performance won't and shouldn't be your primary concern. What's more, sometimes creating prollyfills for experimental APIs requires us to do bad things to HTML, JavaScript, and CSS in order to create something halfway functional, and these bad things often cause performance to fly right out the window. Chalk this up to another reason that access to those "low-level APIs" described in the Extensible Web Manifesto are so critical, as these would allow developers to build prollyfills that also perform reasonably well. Until then, we do the best we can.

But just because performance isn't your primary concern when building a prollyfill doesn't mean it shouldn't be a concern at all. While I don't recommend spending time building comparative JSPerf tests and mining your browser's developer tools in an effort to squeeze out that extra few dozen milliseconds of speed, it is important to pay at least some attention to how your library performs, and apply common sense practices to its construction.

One of the best ways to pay attention to performance in any project, including a prollyfill, is by taking a test-driven development approach to adding features. I've used this approach throughout this book. The basic idea is to first write a failing test for new functionality, to write just enough code to make that test pass, and finally, to consider any refactoring that needs to take place in order to improve the code.

The last step is critical, and I've shown you examples of it in both this chapter and Chapters 4 and 5. On the surface, refactoring might seem like an ascetic preference, but much of the time, the work I put in to improve the code also improves its performance. By removing duplication and looking for opportunities for reuse in my code, I'm encouraging myself to pay attention to ways to also improve that code's performance. When building a prollyfill, taking a TDD approach will ensure that your library performs as well as it can.

Over the course of this short book, we've covered a lot of ground. We spent some time early on talking about why polyfills still matter, and I shared some principles for responsible polyfill development. Then, I put those principles in action and walked you through the creation of a polyfill for the HTML5 Forms specification. Finally, we talked about prollyfills and the opportunity that these present for developers to have a tangible impact on the future of the web platform.

It's an exciting time for the web platform, and it's an exciting time to be a frontend developer. More and more, developers are being given an opportunity to step up to the plate and participate in the standardization and browser evolution processes. Building polyfills is just one of the many ways that developers can participate, but it is unique because it is one backed by actual code and experience. It's a powerful tool that I hope you'll consider wielding as we work to extend the Web forward, together.

About the Author

Brandon Satrom has been a web developer for close to 15 years and has worked with countless web technologies and browsers during that time. He's worked as a Microsoft Web Evangelist, and currently serves as the Lead Program Manager for Telerik's Cross-Platform Tools and Services, which includes Kendo UI, a library for building rich, interactive web and hybrid mobile applications with HTML, JavaScript, and CSS. He cowrote *Building Windows 8 Apps with JavaScript*, which was published in January of 2013 (Addison-Wesley Professional).

Colophon

The animal on the cover of *Building Polyfills* is a beech marten (*Martes foina*), a small mammal native to Europe and central Asia. It is also known as a stone marten or white-breasted marten. It is very adaptable: it lives in both open and forested habitats, and is omnivorous. While plants, nuts, and fruit make up a high percentage of their diet, beech martens also eat eggs, mice, rats, and small birds. Occasionally, they will hunt domestic chickens and rabbits.

Beech martens have coarse brown fur and a white patch on their throat and chest. Not including their long bushy tails (which average around 10 inches long), they are usually 16-19 inches long and weigh 3-5 pounds. They are about the size of a house cat, albeit with a more slender body.

The homes of beech martens can be found in rock crevices, abandoned burrows, tree holes, and even nooks within human buildings—they do not dig their own dens. Beech martens are nocturnal, most active between 6 p.m. to midnight. They are typically solitary animals, except during the summer mating season. Male territories often overlap with those of females, allowing them access to multiple potential mates. Kits aren't born until the following spring: implantation is delayed until roughly 230 days after mating, and gestation takes another month.

In the fur trade, beech marten pelts aren't viewed as of high a quality as related species like the pine marten or sable. Nevertheless, they are still hunted in areas where more valuable furred animals aren't present. There is a population of beech martens in North America—particularly, the state of Wisconsin—descended from animals who escaped from a commercial fur farm in the 1940s.

The cover image is from *A History of British Quadrupeds*. The cover fonts are URW Typewriter and Guardian Sans. The text font is Adobe Minion Pro; the heading font is Adobe Myriad Condensed; and the code font is Dalton Maag's Ubuntu Mono.

Have it your way.

Get even more for your money.

Join the O'Reilly Community, and register the O'Reilly books you own. It's free, and you'll get:

- $4.99 ebook upgrade offer
- 40% upgrade offer on O'Reilly print books
- Membership discounts on books and events
- Free lifetime updates to ebooks and videos
- Multiple ebook formats, DRM FREE
- Participation in the O'Reilly community
- Newsletters
- Account management
- 100% Satisfaction Guarantee

Signing up is easy:

1. **Go to: oreilly.com/go/register**
2. **Create an O'Reilly login.**
3. **Provide your address.**
4. **Register your books.**

Note: English-language books only

To order books online:
oreilly.com/store

For questions about products or an order:
orders@oreilly.com

To sign up to get topic-specific email announcements and/or news about upcoming books, conferences, special offers, and new technologies:
elists@oreilly.com

For technical questions about book content:
booktech@oreilly.com

To submit new book proposals to our editors:
proposals@oreilly.com

O'Reilly books are available in multiple DRM-free ebook formats. For more information:
oreilly.com/ebooks

Spreading the knowledge of innovators   oreilly.com

©2010 O'Reilly Media, Inc. O'Reilly logo is a registered trademark of O'Reilly Media, Inc. 00000

CPSIA information can be obtained at www.ICGtesting.com
Printed in the USA
LVOW01s2152190214

374459LV00011B/20/P